Let There Be Art

The Pleasure and Purpose of Unleashing the Creativity within You

RACHEL MARIE KANG

Revell

a division of Baker Publishing Group
Grand Rapids, Michigan

Published by Revell
a division of Baker Publishing Group
PO Box 6287, Grand Rapids, MI 49516-6287
www.revellbooks.com

Printed in the United States of America

Library of Congress Cataloging-in-Publication Data

Names: Kang, Rachel Marie, 1989– author.
Title: Let there be art : the pleasure and purpose of unleashing the creativity within you / Rachel Marie Kang.
Description: Grand Rapids, MI : Revell, a division of Baker Publishing Group, [2022] | Includes bibliographical references.
Identifiers: LCCN 2022001774 | ISBN 9780800740863 (paperback) | ISBN 9780800742447 (casebound) | ISBN 9781493438921 (ebook)
Subjects: LCSH: Creative ability—Religious aspects—Christianity.
Classification: LCC BT709.5 .K36 2022 | DDC 153.3/5—dc23/eng/20220204
LC record available at https://lccn.loc.gov/2022001774

Baker Publishing Group publications use paper produced from sustainable forestry practices and post-consumer waste whenever possible.

22 23 24 25 26 27 28   7 6 5 4 3 2 1

"We need art. And we need books like this one that remind us of the necessity of our creativity and the importance of sharing our gift with the world. Don't miss this important book!"

Jeff Goins, bestselling author of *Real Artists Don't Starve*

"Rachel Marie Kang gives us a beautiful look at life, beauty, and creativity in *Let There Be Art*. It is a salve to the soul and a call to see the world through new eyes. It is a triumph!"

Alli Worthington, author, speaker, and founder of The Coach School

"*Let There Be Art* is an invitation to rediscover the joy in your life. With poeticism and fierce kindness, Rachel Marie Kang guides us to put pen to paper or paint to canvas to step toward our lives like masterpieces in the making. It is rare for a book to be both deeply beautiful and practical, but, like the best art, Kang's words draw you close. Reader, dare to let there be art."

K.J. Ramsey, licensed professional counselor and author of *This Too Shall Last* and *The Lord is My Courage*

"*Let There Be Art* is not just an anthem for art; it's an anthem for living. I got lost in these pages in the very best way, and then—even better—found. Rachel's poetic, lyrical voice draws you in like a song. You cannot help but dance. I closed this book and immediately opened my journal, wildly inspired to create something beautiful myself."

Ashlee Gadd, founder of Coffee + Crumbs and author of *Create Anyway*

"In her debut book, Rachel Marie Kang helps us see all the ways we create and why our Creator calls it good. Chapter by chapter, Rachel shows us why what we make matters and how, in our making, we join our Maker and fulfill our divine purpose to reflect his creativity.

"My favorite part of this beautiful work is the gift Rachel offers at the end of each chapter through prompts. Each one intended to help us think and feel, remember and imagine—all the while, inspiring us to listen to and follow our hearts' desire to make a favorite recipe, write a letter or a poem, paint a landscape, develop an idea, or sway and dance to music that stirs our souls. And in doing so, respond to God's invitation to create with him, to heed and hear his call to let there be art in our hearts, in our homes, in our communities and churches, and in the world in which we live."

Renee Swope, award-winning and bestselling author
of *A Confident Heart* and *A Confident Mom*

"Rachel Marie Kang has a beautiful way of compiling so much of our humanity and experiences that can cause pain and heartbreak and molds it into something beautiful and impactful. *Let There Be Art* is a liturgy of healing and restoration for the artist soul and gives a breath of fresh air for beginning again—whatever that means for you."

Arielle Estoria, poet, author, actor, artist

"Rachel Marie Kang's debut book breathes life back into the hesitant artist, reminding us all that though we are dust, we are to reflect a glimmer of hope in this dark world. Whether we are wielding words or painting palettes, singing songs, or crafting characters, we were made to make and point back to the Maker of makers."

Meredith McDaniel, licensed professional counselor
and author of *In Want + Plenty*

"Rachel Marie Kang's words make me feel seen and remind me that I am not alone. In her stunning new book, *Let There Be Art*, Rachel awakens us to the God-breathed creative soul that is in each of us and shows us how to stoke that artistic fire so we can pass light onto others. Through richly detailed stories and breathtaking poetry, this book inspires us in our everyday lives to keep going and to keep creating, because it deeply, deeply matters."

Christine Marie Bailey, regenerative farmer and
author of *The Kindred Life*

"Rachel Marie Kang has written a must-read for all creatives. Her glorious approach to prose will carry you from the depths of personal suffering to the fulfillment of God's purpose in your life. Like a warm blanket, *Let There Be Art* will envelop you in comfort and beauty, filling your soul and illuminating your path. Rachel has created a road map to enlightenment, showing how your art, and all art, can bring healing . . . moving us toward light and hope. Rachel provides inspiration to expand our creative dreams along with practical prompts and practices that will make those dreams a reality."

Beth Bell, executive director of BraveWorks

"*Let There Be Art* calls us to find beauty in brokenness. As a writer and speaker, I felt inspired and encouraged by Rachel Marie Kang's invitation to rediscover our creative callings and to co-create art with our Artist God. Though our bodies and souls ache with the darkness, perhaps our art-lived-faith can become the light this world needs."

Michelle Ami Reyes, vice president of the Asian American Christian Collaborative and author of *Becoming All Things*

"Whether we possess a bit of something or are left with nothing at all, one thing is always true: we will create; we will make; we will build. Turning it over and over again in the cycle of creation like our Creator God in whose image we've been made, our art is the very act of calling forth those things that are not as though they were. As our spiritual guide, Rachel calls us back to this holy work of creation, to a place where our art is refined in the light of the one it seeks to illuminate so that we and all who take it in can see that it is good."

Jevon Bolden, founder and CEO of Embolden Media Group and author of *Pray Hear Write*

"The God of the Bible is at once everywhere and elusive, ever present and yet sometimes so very hard to find. For seekers whose words echo the psalmist's cry, 'My soul pants for Thee, O God!' Rachel Marie Kang's *Let There Be Art* is a cup of cool water in a dry and thirsty land. *Let There Be Art* is an astonishing book. Kang's writing has a lyrical quality that pulls the reader along from one chapter to the next, reaching crescendos in prayers and poems that challenge the mind and stir the heart. Her examples from art and culture encourage a reframing of the mind that helps us consider all of life as a reflection of the divine spark we carry within us. Her personal stories draw us in so we feel that her family becomes our family, her experiences become our own experiences. *Let There Be Art* helps readers longing for God uncover a thousand different avenues for finding God's creative beauty and divine presence in the people around us and their own reflection of the image of God. In *Let There Be Art*, Rachel Marie Kang has taken on the role of the Good Samaritan, stooping to bind wounded souls and offer hope for better times to come."

Jeffery M. Leonard, PhD, associate professor of
Biblical Studies at Samford University and
author of *Creation Rediscovered*

"As an art historian, I look at, analyze, and research art daily. But sometimes I need someone like Rachel Marie Kang to call me into art, to see both the beauty and the wonder of daily rhythms and the soul-shuddering ache of our own stories. Art is not the realm of the elites; it generates in all of us as image bearers. In *Let There Be Art*, Rachel weaves a gentle, coaxing invitation to be attentive and welcoming to our own creativity. Drawing together memoir, prayers, and poetry, she prompts us to ask, to seek, and to make. This is the kind of book that you want to read aloud slowly and repeatedly, letting her words both soothe and prick our most tender places."

Elissa Yukiko Weichbrodt, PhD, associate professor
of art and art history at Covenant College

"Rachel's book reminded me that while our identities as 'creatives' can sometimes be sidelined as nonessential, every single one of us was created by the Creator! Creating things is at the core of who we are because it's at the core of who God is. To be alive is to create! Savor each of these pages slowly and feel yourself come alive with her encouragement!"

Aarti Sequeira, TV personality, cook, journalist, and author

To my Creator:

Your works are the most magnificent.
Your art is the most astonishing.
I love you for your miracles,
and I love you for your mysteries.

All of this is *from* you, and *for* you.

Amen.

Contents

Foreword

As many people before me have done, I've turned to writing in search of answers—or at least a sense of camaraderie in the black ink reflected back to me on the page. The words in that season felt like the equivalent of a baby's first steps out into the world. And somehow, all in grace, I found just enough courage to share these words online. I started sharing as a way of checking off the box of stepping into adulthood. I started sharing as a way of trying to find a way to breathe in the world. But then, I received so much more.

I received countless opportunities to practice courage. I received boundless grace that gave me the freedom to let art find its way through my heart, my hands, and out into the world. I also received true friendship. And one of those dearest friends from very early on in this journey is the author of this beautiful, timely book: Rachel Marie Kang.

I don't think it's any coincidence that Rachel and I first met through writing all those years ago. Writing is a practice that many people (such as myself) approached because we wondered if we might be alone in how we felt. Through this very medium, we begin to find belonging and the freedom to strengthen the muscle of having something to say—even if it means doing it while afraid.

When I decided to practice unleashing my creativity, I was one of those people who began to find that sense of belonging. Rachel was one of those friends who helped me find it.

Not too long ago, Rachel and I sat across from each other for lunch after we hadn't seen each other in person for years. However, despite the years and miles between us, it felt like we had just seen each other a few days ago. The last time we saw each other, we were living in different places, we weren't parents yet, we weren't published authors yet, and we hadn't learned how to live through a global pandemic. So much time had passed and yet, it felt like no time had passed at all because the stories, experiences, and creativity that connect us are not bound to time at all. This is the power of *Let There Be Art*. It's not just social media posts and books; it's a daily opportunity to be fully a part of creation—then join in on creating every day in subtle and grand ways.

I am so grateful for the friendship I share with Rachel, and I am also grateful for how it has become a grace-filled reminder of how wonderful it is when you live from a place of knowing you were made to create. You just never know what will happen when you finally allow all that has been stirring within you to come to life. You can never know who you will meet, what new things will be revealed to you, and how you will grow. But you can know this: it matters to come forth into the light. It matters to spend time exploring and nurturing the creative within and, as Rachel says, to "join God in creating." This book will help you do just that. Now is the time to create. Now is the time to join in. There is so much waiting to be revealed to you within these pages and beyond.

Morgan Harper Nichols, artist, poet, and author of
All Along You Were Blooming *and* Peace Is a Practice

Invitation

May Your Light Break Forth

The idea for this book came in the dark of night while nursing my newborn and crying into my shoulder from sheer exhaustion. The pitching of this book came while pregnant in the middle of the COVID-19 pandemic, while all the world was cradling a collective trauma—the shared sorrows that came in the moments and months following the unjust death of George Floyd. The writing of this book came in the endless weeks spent oscillating from doctor to doctor, swimming in a sea of unseen symptoms caused by a nodule in my neck, wreaking havoc on my health.

When *you* finally find yourself ready to sit down at your desk to write, or in that studio to paint, or in that sanctuary to speak, or at that sunrise wedding to photograph, or on that stage to dance, or in that shed to make, or in your living room to play piano, or in that classroom to theorize, or in your kitchen to chop thyme or cilantro or parsley or any other herb you need to make that recipe from your grandmother's treasured cookbook, or wherever it is that you stand or kneel or walk or sit to create and cause beauty to be and beam from the hollow of your hands—you will find that everything, and I mean *everything*, will rise up against you.

Every holy, hard, and impossible thing will rise up to greet you, will shake hands with you, will remind you of the painful truth that has been true of every beautifully created being since the beginning of time.

The truth is that none of this is easy—none of our living, none of our loving, and certainly none of our longing to create. You will come to question, just like I have, if it really is the right time to consider writing a book, or taking up pottery, or plotting a garden, or homeschooling your children between the small walls of your borrowed home.

You will question, just like I have, if it is okay to say that you are a maker, or a writer, or an artist, or the ever-elusive creative, whatever in the world that means. You will question whether the work of your hands has worth, whether you can call the things you do and make *art*, and whether you really can claim that all of it is meaningful and irrevocably needed by others.

I imagined you would find yourself in this curious place of questioning. In a place of wondering if the cosmos really is parting wide open and welcoming you to partake in the age-old practice of wielding wonder and making things. I knew that you would find yourself in a place of wanting to make things, not merely for the sake of making a name for yourself, but more so for the fact that not doing so might reduce you to an exhale, a breath that came into this world and quickly departed.

I knew that you might sometime find yourself in a place of pondering the possibility that your existence on this tilting planet may be less about making a mark on this world and more about having a mark made in *you*.

For whatever reason, however inconspicuously the thoughts came seeping in, there is a deeply embedded string of beliefs that you, that we all—collectively—have come to accept as truth. We've come to believe that meaningful things come easy and that beautiful things can only come from an elite few. That pretty poems can only come from the pens of published poets. That a ballerina can only practice pliés for the sake of perfection but not for sheer pleasure. That breathtaking concertos can only come from Brahms and Bach but not from the skilled hands of contemporary composers.

I do not know why I rise and wake with a desire deep down in my soul to dismantle these beliefs, to join with those who have gone before me—Makoto Fujimura, Madeleine L'Engle, Andrew Peterson, Sho Baraka—and attempt to unravel the many ways we've succumbed to living like there is any reason to believe that beautiful, meaningful, honest things—*that art*—cannot, in fact, rise up from that which is broken, imperfect, unseen, or unsure.

The truth is, I cannot tell you why the lungs within you heave with weakness. I cannot tell you why the life growing within you could not become bones and body enough to sustain breath. I cannot tell you why the gut-wrenching loneliness that you feel steals your hope, why the hurt burns so bad that you can barely lift your body from the couch to live another day.

Nor can I tell you why palettes of paint speak to you, why it always seems to be that nature calls out to you, like some grand invitation. I cannot tell you why you feel alive, so impossibly alive, when you sing, or bake, or tell stories in auditoriums before one hundred eager hearts. I cannot tell you how and why these swells of grief and joy come to you the way that they do.

I can only tell you how to make the most of them, how to make the most of what you know and who you are. I can tell you that, in the grand scheme of things, it really does matter to see the work of your hands as worthy.

It matters to believe that every journal entry, every captured photograph, every scale practiced, and every letter penned drip and drown with more weight and wonder than you will ever come to possibly imagine or understand.

In his book *Creativity*, the late Mihaly Csikszentmihalyi talks about the ancient Roman saying *libri aut liberi*, which conveys the inevitable and difficult choice between living to raise children or living to write books.[1] This saying memorializes a cultural concept that still exists today and implies the impossibility of successfully centering one's own life around creativity *as well as* family, community, intimacy, and legacy. This way of thinking, so ancient and yet still prevalent today, begs us to believe that the way of creativity is quintessential and clean—that it cannot be a collision of all that is hard and hopeful.

I have pondered this ancient saying, have thought deeply and widely about it, looking at my own life and the lives of those I know and love. I see the many ways that we sketch, self-publish books, try new recipes, create costumes from scratch, and build businesses with our bare hands.

All of this, while simultaneously tending to children, tending to careers, and tending to lists and needs and aches and ailments that pull at us from every which way.

When I see these chaotic collisions, I cannot help but say that *this* is how it's meant to be. It's never going to be *libri aut liberi*, one or the other. It's never going to be easy without the hard, joyful without the grief, magical without the mundane, light without the dark, or art without the struggle.

In your creating, even in your enjoyment of what *others* create, there will always be wars to wage and work to do—fears to fend off, children or communities to care for, lies to unlearn, and evil to overcome.

I see you now, coming to the last line of the last chapter, turning loose the last page and releasing yourself from the spell and spine of this book. I see you sighing with relief and then saying to yourself that it is time to step into a new place. A place of permission, a place of embracing. A place of cultivating the courage to speak into the void of your own heart. A place in which you find yourself professing and proclaiming your acceptance of all the dreams and words and ideas that swell within.

I imagine you returning to this book, time and time again, to be reminded of all the ways that creativity lends itself to you. In these pages, you will find a woven tapestry of quotes and references to art in its various forms. You will find fragments of my story, creative writing, and the unraveling of biblical truths.

It is not enough to simply share my story, however. It is not even enough for Bible verses to be peppered in and through these pages. For the words in this book to sink in deep, they must be felt, seen, tasted, and heard. After all, art itself is tangible—incarnate.

Therefore, this book must *show* as much as it tells.

For this very reason, you will find poems and pieces by people I admire, as well as people who are a part of my online creative community, Fallow Ink. Like paint on canvas, these poems and pieces give color to the concepts this book explores.

Might the words in this book read like a play on a stage, like a curtain being pulled open ever so gently, leaving you to see something so spectacular that you can't help but walk away singing the songs, can't help but walk away changed.

Use these prompts to prick your heart to think and feel. Let them stir the ideas, stories, and truths within you. Answer these prompts any way that you wish. Write about them in a journal or share your thoughts in a post online. Let inspiration lead you to create a recipe, to write letters to your grandparents or children, to read a new fiction book, to start singing, to create characters, and to write scripts. Let the answering of these prompts awaken a new day, a new world within you—or, perhaps, an old world begging to come to life again.

This is a kaleidoscopic call, a wild and messy welcome for you to let light break forth from every darkest corner, for a new dawn to rise over any shadow of darkness in your heart, in your home, in your life, and in this world.

For the sake of irresistible pleasure and irrevocable purpose, *create* with me and *come* with me to heed and hear the call to let there be art.

> You are not just a body of bones and blood and breath,
> you are a heart bending to hear,
> you are a soul straining to see something
> beautiful in the midst of all that breaks.

> And, there will never be enough time or courage or certainty
> to write out all you wonder about,
> to make art of all you sense and see.

> But there is faith.

> There is showing up, anyway.
> There is standing before the canvas,
> or the computer, or the clay
> even when you feel rushed and unsure,
> bruised and broken.

> Even while you are seeking and stumbling,
> fumbling to find your way through.

And, this is bravery.

That you might come to call this kind of
breathtaking curiosity, beautiful.

That you might dare call it creativity,
dare call this swell of wonder within you

art.

Let There Be Bareness

Write what disturbs you, what you fear, what you have not been willing to speak about. Be willing to be split open.

— Natalie Goldberg, *Writing Down the Bones*

There I am, in that four-by-six-inch frame forever etched in my mind. A brown girl, standing under a sun-stretched sky, seeing clear through the bright of it, staring deep into the burn of it. *It is Easter.*

And I am clutching a brown, boxed-up bunny. But beneath the hand-stitched dress is a candy-coated bitter of my own—a boxed-up beating heart banging on the bones of my rib cage.

There, in that 1997 Kodak memory, I am not just the girl with chocolate; I am the girl with *a lot.* The girl who carries a lot. The girl who questions a lot. The girl who can't help but see that her lot in life is always an asking, but never an answering. Never a knowing, never a clearing of the confusion that fills up every crevice of her childlike, need-to-know soul.

21

I was just a young girl when I learned how to see brokenness more than any other thing.

I looked for it, even when I could not name it—in the ruin of run-down buildings, in flowers faltering and failing to bloom. I did more than just see brokenness. I *sensed* it, could feel it sweeping around me, seeping in and out of me. The young girl that I was, so good at gathering broken things and burying them deep within, until I was no longer just beholding brokenness, but it was beholding me.

Brokenness *becoming* me.

This is the beginning I remember. My seven-year-old soul, already giving in to the lie that life always leaves the living lost, lifeless, and without light. Already bending to believe the worst about the world and the worst about the ones she loved.

Even, especially, the worst about herself.

But this is all of our beginnings, is it not? We all come breaking out through birth—all baby breath and broken cries—desperate and in need of someone to hold our heaving, heavy selves. We come out crying into the chaos of our world, wary with the inhale of brokenness, the heavy birthright that it seems to be.

"There isn't one of us who isn't cut right from the beginning," writes Ann Voskamp. "All of us get pushed from safe wombs out into this holy mess. All of us need someone to catch us and hold us right from the beginning, and for one sacred moment, every single one of us is cupped. And then they cut that one thick umbilical cord. You can spend a lifetime feeling pushed out, cut off, abandoned—inexplicably alone."[1]

All of this is true, all of us are born into this brokenness. All of us are birthed and brought into this earth of inevitable darkness, a darkness that burns beneath the bone.

A story that began before man's first breath was ever an exhale.

―――――

You already know the story of a serpent hissing whispers of shame, of the forbidden fruit and the inevitable fall of man. So, instead of telling you about the woman and man taking a bite and indelibly breaking the heart of God, I will tell you the story of *God's* breaking—of God breaking up the darkness and bringing forth light.

It's the story of God staring out into an abyss, a great, magnificent nothing, to which he speaks, "Let there be light" (Gen. 1:3). Time and space stand still as he wills the suspension of celestial light to push back the boundaries of darkness.

He laces land around the wild waters, calls the work of his hands *good*, and readies the world to sustain life while this new light shines forth.

It is *here*, long before our breath and bodies came into being, where our stories begin. It is *here*, where the looming possibility of the incredibly hard and terrible things that happen in our lives first lingers.

Our story first begins with the fold of darkness, not with the forbidden fruit and the inevitable fall. Our story begins when God creates boundaries to contain and control the darkness and the deep. It begins with the world that God calls *good* but that he still allows to remain with "a sense of wildness and chaos that must yet be controlled."[2]

God, in his infinite power, plans a partnership with man in this work of pushing back the darkness, long before he even breathes life into man's lungs.

Jeffery M. Leonard, PhD, Hebrew Bible scholar and associate professor of Biblical Studies at Samford University, writes that

"God charges humankind with taking up the divine mantle of creating and working to push back the boundaries of this chaos still further."[3]

It is within this tension, this controlled chaos that has not been completely cast away, that God ultimately initiates *tikkun olam*, a Judaic concept that defines this tension as God's purpose of leaving room for repair in this world. A plan that God invites us to participate in, a work of pushing back the darkness in this world, of tending to this wild planet, of tending to our own wild hearts, and of being a part of restoring all things to the way they could and should be.

To peace.

God's plan wasn't simply to save us from the inevitability of sin. His desire all along was that we would live and long to push back the darkness, *just like him*, forever holding our gaze upon *his* goodness and *his* great light.

The truth about the creation story is that man was not the only one to fall into temptation. Beneath the story of man's fall into sin is that of Satan's—an angelic being created by God to shine with light and goodness who, instead of pushing back the darkness in his own heart, gives way to it.

Then, darkness begets.

Eve, the tempted, becomes the temptress.

When faced with the choice of life and light or death and disunion with God, she and Adam stand there, two bodies, bare and unbelieving. They forsake faith and they bite into the fruit. They fall with the fate of every human heart on their fingers.

They didn't just break a set of rules.

They broke their hearts open to Satan's unbounded way of being. They broke their hearts wide open to a way of life that pushes back the light and love *of* God instead of pushing back the dark *with* God.

Brokenness wasn't our beginning. We began as breath bound to the heartbeat of God.

We were not damned from the beginning. Darkness was.

We were not bad and broken from the beginning. We were believed in from the beginning.

We began, not prone to wander but prone to worship.

Our natural-born bent wasn't for sin and sorrow. It was for the sound and the song of God.

But there, in the garden, we traded the sound and song of God, the whispering of his love, for the wrenching lie of Satan. And the broken pieces in us have been straining to hear and know the difference between the two ever since.

It is no wonder that we hide, that we hush the whispers within that call us to create.

We, in our fallen state, are broken; we believe the worst about ourselves.

That is what darkness does when it goes without being pushed back. It lies. It hides all that is good and true. All that is light and life.

Giving in to the lies, we fear the perpetuation of what happened in the garden. We fear we might hear and heed the wrong whisper again. We fear we might listen to a lie and cause a downfall, a destruction to last beyond the length of our lives.

And yet, the one thing we need is the one thing we avoid.

Art.

Art, not as a way of claiming that we are right about anything, but *art* as a way of climbing back toward the light. Yes, *art* as a way of pushing back the darkness within ourselves, within our world.

This art can be *anything* good that comes from our hands. Madeleine L'Engle writes that there really is no such thing as good or bad art. There is only good religion or bad religion, both of which influence the nature of the art.[4]

There is only creativity that lends itself to recreating chaos or there is creativity that lends itself to bringing order and redemption in the world.

All art *is* art. A song is a song, a sketch is a sketch, a sidewalk full of chalk drawings is a sidewalk full of chalk drawings. The matter isn't whether these things bear some sort of measurable amount of beauty; rather, it's whether the art helps us name that which is ineffable. It's whether the art tells the truth about the goodness of God—whether it speaks to and awakens you, turns the light on in the dark corners of your heart.

Any and *all* art that helps, heals, names, entertains, or redeems *is* good.

By and through art, we are led out of hiding and into *hereness*—out of obscurity and into the obvious. Art invites us to stand before God, naked and vulnerable. Broken and bare. Unclothed, unhidden, and uncovered.

Leafless, as we always should have been.

I have a coir, stitched welcome mat by the door that reads: *Bare your soles.*

As in, bare your soles but also bare that actual *soul* of yours. Smooth out that wrinkle on your forehead, calm your beating heart, and come to stillness, to presence.

The mat at my front door is like a welcome sign that beckons bystanders to walk and enter through, all barefoot and barely breathing, all desperate for a couch to catch their tired bodies.

I cannot help but think of how the same is true of a blank page, or a blank canvas, or an empty stage—they are all the invitation that bids:

Come. Bare your soul.

On the blank canvas or page or stage, when it is only your eyes that peer and perceive, you are welcome to create. You are welcome to bare your heart, the very words buried within.

You can create in confidence, all while withholding criticism, as you work through the wandering and the wondering of your soul.

Thinking back to the garden, to our beginning, it's so vital to know that God's call for man to bravely bring his heart was not meant to instill condemnation. Rather, it was to distill confession.

In Genesis 3, God calls to man asking, "Where are you? . . . Who told you that you were naked? . . . What is this you have done?" (vv. 9, 11, 13).

These questions, these invitations to tell truth, are God presenting his presence. It is God establishing himself as an eternal audience of one, ever listening and leaning into the laments of our living, loving, and losing.

God is still that safe place—indeed, he is the safest. And he welcomes our stories, our honest words and artful, paint-filled songs and poems and posts and pieces. For they are the utterances of our traveling souls, utterances that he himself will never undermine or undercut.

We matter.

Our minds, hearts, bodies, and souls matters. Every detail divulged and every inexpressible, wordless groan matters. He is present *in* and he is pleased *by* the process of our hearts honestly and artfully pouring out before his.

Maybe it's true for all of us.

Maybe we long to create not just for the ridding, but for a filling of some kind. To be told a truth that we can take with us all through life, a sound speaking over the noise of the world.

A hope that, by shining light on our shattered hearts, piece by piece, they might be put back together again.

Could it be that the spinning together of words with black ink on blank pages might help make sense of all that doesn't make sense in the world? Could it be that baking cakes and stretching limbs long toward lofty skies might help release peace into every unseen piece of our lives?

We write that we might experience the exhale of God again, the sigh and sound of his voice that reminds us of his plan to fill our lives with light.

I see you now, taking everything within you to the page, to posts shared with the world. I see you, no longer fumbling behind coverings or hiding in shame. No longer feeling pushed out by darkness but brought into light.

In writing, you can create with and through words. You can build a new and beautiful world in which the wild and the dark will no longer overpower or overshadow you. In the beautiful words of Lore Wilbert Ferguson:

> Tell me, I want to say to my fellow writers, tell me of your inner demons, tell me of your flesh. I want to hear the war that waged within you as you navigated complex stories and spaces. I want to know how hard you fought and how much you wept and

how little you prayed. Tell it honest, tell it slant, tell it however you want to, but tell the truth because the truth is ten thousand little protests that got you where you are and every one of them matters to God and to me and even to you because there you are and there you were all along.[5]

It is not only God who beckons bare words from you, it's me. It's the world. It's the ones around you who know you. It's you deeply wanting to brave your soul and bring your beating heart.

Yes, by way of words you can stand bare before a God who does not badger or beat the truth out of you. He is a gentle, whispering God standing with you, not against you, through it all. He moves you to breathe—a slow seeping, a brave release to gradually push back your darkest memories and moments.

God calls *for* you but also comes *to* you. Telling you that it is okay to bare all of who you are. That you can live beyond brokenness, and that you can become new in spite of it.

You need not sustain or suffer any wild or dark force in your life or in this world. You can safely, artfully name what is good.

And you can surely call out and cast away that which is not.

There he is.

There God *always* is, covering you.

Not with some withering leaf, but with his everlasting love.

Prayer

God, let me hear the sound and song of your love over the lies. Help me to step out of hiding and into honest hereness. Awaken bravery as I bare my brokenness. Shine a light onto my wounds, and release your healing into the world. Let it be so, in and through me. Amen.

Prompts

What makes your heart beat?

What makes your heart break?

Practices

Light a candle, pour yourself a cup of something soothing, and skim through old journals, letters, emails, or text messages. Read the entries. Observe the dates. Notice your handwriting. Admire the honesty. Reminisce about all you've lived through and how far you've come. Reflect on old wounds, worries, and the wars of the world—all those things that made (and still make) life hard. Then, write in a journal, or a note on your phone, or a letter, or a social media post on how baring honest words in particular seasons of your life has brought you to become who you are today.

Buy a new journal if you need a new start. Make a moment, a big deal out of it. It isn't a failure to have unfinished journals. It is noble to begin again. May opening to the blank page of a brand-new journal help you take new steps toward opening your heart to honesty, self-awareness, and truth.

Pieces

I tried to pick myself up off the floor,
but every time I tried,
my broken self would grip a shard
that cut me deep and cried:
I am broken. I'm not beautiful. Who could ever love
  this mess?
Until, somehow, Love Himself came down
and did what Love does best.

—Katherine Nadene

Doubt pools in the softness
between my folded fingers,
like rain beneath
a broken gutter.
My faith is flooded.
Unfinished prayer dries
on my tongue.

But God whispers:

Bring Me your doubt.
This too, is part
of worship, to come exactly
as you are. And this, too,
is a way of healing,
to find I love you
just the same.

—Gina Sares

Let There Be Goodness

The pleasure of the table belongs to all ages, to all conditions, to all countries . . . it mingles with all other pleasures, and remains at last to console us for their departure.

—Jean Anthelme Brillat-Savarin, *The Physiology of Taste*

Any one of my cousins, aunts, or uncles can tell you about Grandma's couch—how you sink right into it, sink deep into the embroidered flowers that look borrowed from upholstery.

Grandma's house.

My memory takes me there when I am sifting through the moments in my life that gathered goodness. There we are—Mom, brothers, aunts, uncles, and every cousin in between—in that small living room, all of us hugged by soft green walls and kissed by light seeping in through sheer curtains.

Grandma's house is the center from which my childhood memories hold, all those holidays spent hanging silver tinsel on green trees and catching crayfish in the creek that crackled under the bridge.

I know by heart every corner of that house, tucked into the woods and beneath the mountains. I lived there, for a time, after my parents split and sold our second house. And I will never forget it, never forget our clothes packed in big cardboard boxes or the piles of everything else we owned, all stuffed in big, black plastic bags.

There is a memory I hold on to from the time I spent living there. My grandma, sitting in her favorite recliner, calling out.

"Rachel," she says. "Come here. I think you'll like this."

"Is it a recipe?" I ask, thinking about how it's *always* a recipe.

"Not a recipe this time. Just something I saw," she tells me.

She grabs a loose piece of scrap paper and writes out S-H-M-I-L-Y. Then, she holds out the note to me and leaves me to guess the pronunciation.

"Shh-my-lee?" I ask.

"Shh-mill-ee," she replies.

She tells me that it is a game for two people to write secret notes in surprise places.

In dust on tables.

In rolls of toilet paper.

In steam on bathroom mirrors.

In corners of Christmas cards.

She tells me how the very meaning of the word, *See How Much I Love You*, is an invitation to search, seek, and see. A *shmily* here, on a note left on the tiled kitchen table. A *shmily* there, in a birthday card or traced into the dust on the coffee table. It was our little game, like leaving letters lost at sea. Only they weren't lost.

And neither were we.

Like the sweet surprise of *shmily* notes tucked away in the most unassuming of places, goodness is a gift that has to be found. To *see* goodness is to *seek* goodness. It is a lifelong grasping for glimpses of good things that ground us to God.

The truth is that goodness surrounds us to the point that we should be astounded. The problem isn't that we are short of goodness, it's that we do not know how to see it hiding in plain sight. We do not know how to see it in the dust on tables, in rolls of toilet paper, in steam on bathroom mirrors.

It just might be that this is because, in life, we often look for the bad more than we look for the good. We look for the hard that we know by heart, and we hold our gaze on the things that hurt.

But there is something that I must whisper to you, something I must say before you come to the last, thin pages at the end of this book. You must know that this chapter is so vitally important, because if you miss learning the art of seeing goodness, then you will miss the gifts that have always been yours.

You will miss the way of God.

You will miss living wide-eyed in wonder.

You will miss seeing, *really seeing*, the world around you—the *ones* around you.

The most generous thing you can do for yourself is give yourself time. There are layers to finding goodness. You will not be scratching the surface.

Goodness can be found in the car rides with your grandfather while he tells you stories about moving the kids from one house to another. It can be the standstill of time when you snuggle up next to your son as he burns the eraser through sheets of loose-leaf paper. It's the resiliency you feel as you make that daily run. It's the distant sound of church bells and your favorite childhood playground, the friends with freckled faces you won't soon forget.

Goodness is in all the moments you never thought to note as noteworthy; it's in the memories that saved themselves into your soul.

It's in the family meals that tell the story of who you are.

A story that no one else can tell but you.

Some of the most prevalent and prominent memories we hold involve food. This is because eating, as Chef José Andrés says, "is one thing, besides breathing, that we all do from the day we are born until the day we die."[1]

Many of my childhood memories that hold goodness take place around the table—spoonfuls of Grandma's chicken and dumplings, Aunt Luwaine's scalloped potatoes, and Uncle Junior and Aunt Donna's platters of venison.

I will never forget growing up and pressing plantains deep into frying pans, or the golden *tostones* I ate at Bocas del Toro in Panama. I still taste the German sunflower seed bread I tried in Großhansdorf, served with black coffee and toppings like ghee.

I'll always remember the cooking class I took with my cousin Tiara and how we learned to crack open cloves of garlic with the flat of a knife, the pungent aroma seeping deep into our pores.

These are the memories I cannot seem to forget, and I know they are the kind you also carry. You cannot ever say that you have never tasted goodness. Someone cooked for you, sprinkled a thick layer of adobo seasoning on *arroz con pollo* for you. Someone slipped strawberry bonbons into the empty pockets of your winter coat. Someone—a parent, a teacher, a friend of a friend—taught you how to stir soup, chop cold carrots, and slice onions until you wept.

You have tasted and you have seen—from stove-top ramen to grilled cheese to fine cuisine. You have mumbled grace at the table of one thousand modest meals, all bursting with color and culture and creativity.

What a gift, *what goodness*, that the food you eat and the meals you make are inherently creative. What a gift that God would make our lives fulfilled by something that *gives* us fill.

When it comes to creativity, you can say that you are no painter—that you are no poet, no award-winning actor, no chef de cuisine. But one thing you are is a human with a hunger that burns for flavor and food. You are a father cooking for your kids. You are a volunteer making meals for moms. You are an experimental baker, a chocolatier, a coffee connoisseur, all in your own right.

You are making magic in the mundane, slicing mushrooms and sprinkling salt. You are not just cooking, you are *creating*. With every meal, you're not just taking in food—you are *tasting* food.

Aarti Sequeira writes that cooking is holy ground to experience God. She writes that a friend of hers taught her how to pray before she cooks, and how this simple practice led her down a path that changed the way that she viewed her food.

> Flipping through a book on Ayurveda, the ancient Indian system of medicine, I learned that not only is food our medicine but also its preparation. Chopping vegetables is a moving meditation, soothing our minds and bodies. God tucked medicine even into the mundane.[2]

When I first read these words by Aarti on the (in)courage blog, it brought chills to my skin and up my spine. Aarti put words to something I was sensing, something I believe we all sense deep down inside.

In my own life, after weeks of ordering takeout at the start of the COVID-19 pandemic, I had found that my hands missed all the touch and texture that preparing food has to offer.

My hands had missed bagging broccolini and brussels sprouts. I missed the color of carrots and slicing fresh lemon. I missed scooping out the flesh of butternut squash and cooking it down into an autumn soup, seasoned with cinnamon and topped with sage.

In an effort to avoid stress in the first weeks of the pandemic, I sacrificed the slow and creative act of chopping vegetables—a practice with the potential to nourish attention and cultivate calm.

Aarti's words called me to, once again, stop and see the colors of freshly chopped vegetables. Her words reminded me not to miss a moment of giving thanks for the generosity of our God, of the good planet he created and the good food he gave us.

The meals we make and the food we taste are but one way to cultivate creativity in the midst of the mundane—to see beauty, to tell stories, to gather, and to take care of friends and family, of *ourselves*.

Baking, blessing meals, even bagging groceries are all simple and creative ways to keep seeing, feeling, touching, tasting, and hearing the goodness of our world, as well as the goodness of the ones around us.

This is a kind of art that will always surround us, meal by meal, bite by bite.

Breath by breath.

Prayer

God, slow me down to smell the spices. Open my eyes to see goodness in the food I make and the food I taste. Help me to see goodness in the gathering of people around my table, in the chopping of every colorful vegetable. Teach me how to tend to the earth, to give thanks for what it gives to me. Whisper wonder to me when I am weary from cooking. Nourish my body, mind, and soul. Amen.

Prompts

If you were an herb, which one would you be?
If you were a spice, which one would you be?

Practices

Use Aarti's advice and pray before you cook. Slow yourself to stillness and pause before you begin. Whisper words under your breath to center and bless your creating. If you cannot come up with your own prayer, use the one above. You can also pray before you shop for groceries or fill the pantry. Pray before you dine in or order out. Make a ritual out of blessing your food (whether you prepare it or not). Thank God for his creative provisions and for the people who play a part in it. Invite friends and family to gather around your table. Host them for holidays and offer to make meals for them in the mundane. You don't have to be a chef or the one cooking. You can serve finger foods. You can order takeout. Give thanks for the friends and family that you have. Let them know you enjoy their company. Collect these moments and cherish your memories of them.

Pieces

Our house is going out to the world today in the form of listings, emails, calls, and texts. We've been flying out the door at a moment's notice already for other people to come walk around inside our home. Our first home. I think about those strangers, how they have no idea two of my children were born in one of those rooms. They don't know the floor is worn with our fears. They don't know which doors were locked in our rage. They don't know how warm were the rooms full of friends. They don't know the walls there have this certain power of protection, like bones nurturing the tender body within to heal, to grow, to live. But then too, I think, I don't know those strangers. I don't know the plans, the gardens, the food, the memories they will make in the house we're leaving. And I think about what home really is and how we're ready to be those strangers, somewhere else. How do you leave something that feels as safe as skin? Gladly, bravely, gratefully.

—Christina Williams

The more I fret, the more I forget,
Your goodness in the land of the living.

The more I see, the more I need,
Your goodness in the land of the living.

The more I taste, the less I waste,
Your goodness in the land of the living.

The more I hear, the less I fear,
Your goodness in the land of the living.

May I not fret and never forget.
May I have eyes to see and always need.
May I choose to taste and never waste.

May I have ears to hear and never fear,
Your goodness in the land of the living.

—Ashley Whittemore

Let There Be Likeness

Nothing can be compared to the great beauty and capabilities of a soul; however keen our intellects may be, they are as unable to comprehend them as to comprehend God, for, as He has told us, He created us in His own image and likeness.

—Saint Teresa of Avila, *The Interior Castle*

There is a memory that I hold hostage, one that lies buried deep beneath the box of my bones. And rarely do I summon it, call to it, think of it. For it reminds me of a time when I tried so desperately to be nothing that I was and everything that I wasn't.

In fragments, the memory comes to me. I am with my dad. He revs the engine of his black Kawasaki motorcycle. He hands me a helmet and I fumble to fit it over my long, thick, mixed hair. I sit behind him and we drive through the familiar streets of where we live.

Spring Valley.

Flashbacks remind me of the Finkelstein Library where, often, my mother walked with my brothers and me. There is the Spring Valley Memorial Park, the firehouse, and the funeral home. Then there is the beauty salon, the place from which this memory stems. A woman smooths white cream into my hair. The smell is strong, it stings and burns, and I'm just breathing through it, just being through it.

The relaxing cream that seared my scalp burned a lie that I learned to believe right down to the bone of me—that I was not good enough to be who I was and that I needed to be what everyone else wanted me to be.

In all of my burning and blow-drying, I tried to conform to the look the world wanted. I grew up learning that the hair on my head was a burden, that the fullness of it was easier to laugh at than to love. I conformed to a worldview that left me reeling and confused, unsure of who and how I was to exist within the world.

How do you believe that you are beloved if the world is bent on burning the way you look?

How do you believe that you are beloved if your eyes are blinded from seeing God's love?

There is this idea in art, this concept, called "The Beholder's Share."[1] And it is this idea that a piece of art is incomplete until meaning is projected by an audience. It's this idea that there is a relationship, an interaction between a work of art and the one beholding it.

A piece of art is named worthy and valuable not only by the artist, the one who created the art, but by its audience, the one *viewing* the art.

What's interesting is every person will perceive a piece of art differently than the next. That is because every person holds their own life experiences and inferences.

This artful concept of "The Beholder's Share" unveils a powerful, actual truth, the idea that we, ourselves—the works of art that we are—are incomplete without the gaze of an audience, a gaze that determines our worth and, ultimately, our purpose.

What is hard, and oftentimes devastating, is that we humans are imperfect. Our experiences are imperfect as is our nature. Just as we have the ability to behold something and say that it is worthy, we also have the propensity to behold something and say that it is *not* worthy.

This is the kind of gaze that holds inferences based on decades of prejudices, the kind of gaze that's led communities and countries to deem people with certain characteristics as not good or not good enough.

So, if our gazing is subject to imperfect preference, then whose gaze matters in the grand scheme of our lives? How do we come to see and believe in our own worth? How do we inhale and exhale beauty? How do we tune and turn our eyes to see ourselves as beloved?

The way is this: we must know that our belovedness as created beings is determined first by the gaze of God—the master artist who first created and gazed upon his creation.

God is both artist *and* audience.

God is both creating art and looking into it and calling it good, giving it worth that precedes the opinions of others.

The one who took dust upon his hand, breathing into it like a prayer, initiated the becoming of us. All of who we are—the color of our skin, the texture of our hair, the slant of our noses, the stretch of freckles across our faces like constellations across the sky—all of this is beautiful and born of his imagination.

We stand wildly beloved and beheld in the gaze of a God who calls us good.

Deeply, He beckons.
Wildly

softly, swiftly.

Like the flapping of a flock,
brushing wind upon the cheek.

Upon the brow,
upon that button of a nose,
upon the heart.

Sweeping in, like
the misty fog,
heavy on mountaintops.

Wrapping us thick in
His presence, in
His hereness.

He,
God. He is
here.

In this moment,
in this now.

And, He is not a bird,
sitting on lofty telephone lines, He

is in flight,
is rushing in,
is every which way.

He is moving, He is moving,
He is moving.

He is moving you, He
is moving me, to
stillness. To

knowingness.

Because He is wild for us,
like the wind, all too
invisible and unseen, but

untamed, for you
and me.

There is nothing in God's being that bases our worth off inferences, or preferences, or experiences, or hand-me-down histories.

He looks lovingly at us and calls us beloved. It isn't lofty at all but is lowly. He is holy but is humbled to be with and for us.

And when we believe in the gaze of God, believe that he created and calls us good, our brains will bend and bow to believe in beauty *beyond* ourselves. We will learn to see the beauty in all of God's people.

We won't just learn to see the good in others.

We will learn to see *God* in others.

The way that we see ourselves is also the way we'll see the world. If we see ourselves as works of art, then we will see everything else around us in the same captivating light. Like a grand awakening, our eyes will bend to see the beauty in the people and places around us. We will see that every being has wonder and worth. With this truth in mind, we will create from the truth of our own createdness.

This is what L'Engle means when she says:

We are human and humble and of the earth, and we cannot create until we acknowledge our createdness.[2]

Understanding this relationship between creator and creation, or artist and audience, opens a world of invitation to see not just beauty but *being*. This makes the difference come time to look beyond the skin and see that, at the core, we look like God.

To deeply know this truth is to release ourselves from trying to become the things that our earthly beholders want us to be. This truth unleashes us to look to the gaze of the one who created us. It brings us to believe that we are the beloved in the eyes of our beholding Father.

We are already works of art, made complete by the God who raised us from dust.

Made by him.

Made to be *like* him.

Our likeness of God goes beyond skin and bone—it goes right down to our being. It goes to our characteristics, our personalities, our wit, our charm, our depth, our ache for community. It goes down to all the many ways in which we live for love and bend toward beauty.

These things are not merely seen in the face of God, but in the heart of God.

Our likeness is like his own, and it is not merely reflected in our faces. Rather, his likeness can be seen in the foundation of *how* we are.

Likeness in art—in portraiture, in caricature, in sculpture, in sketch, in design—is not about focusing on the fine details of features. Likeness in art is about *location*.[3] This means it's not about how you draw, paint, or sketch the details—it's *where* you draw them.

Think about the way a person changes—the way they age through life or how in certain seasons the hair is long or short or different in color. Think of the ways we lose and gain weight and how, though we change, we still look the same.

This is how you can look at photographs of a person from their wedding day and still recognize their face in photographs from fiftieth wedding anniversaries. This is because likeness lies deeper than the surface of skin. Through the years, a person's features change, while their physical proportions—the width of their nose, the distance between their eyes, the length of their chin, their *likeness*—remains the same.

The breathtaking thing about this is how all of us live with the look and likeness of God. Outwardly, our collective communities, countries, and cultures may all look different. But, looking closely, there is likeness. And it is not based on our features—our skin, our language, our genetic predispositions, and whether we're tall or thin.

These details do matter, but they don't determine the origin of our createdness.

In our souls, we look like the one who created us. Therefore, we can *live* like the one who created us. In this, we've been made with the capacity to create—not just works of art, but a *world* that reflects the very nature of our God.

I once took a virtual art class with my friend Rebecca. We were learning how to work with wet clay and, to my surprise, the clay was dry. So dry, I couldn't form it. I couldn't move it or mold it. I could barely roll it or shape it. It took a while, but I finally realized that, somehow, I missed the teacher's instructions that we would need water to smooth and work the clay. Without it, we wouldn't get very far.

I wondered how much I often feel like dry clay myself. I wondered how, sometimes, I find myself getting stuck in the shapes and molds that others make for me.

Sometimes, I need a little smoothing out too.

Sometimes, I need the reminder that God is still forming me.

Sometimes, I need the love of God to wash over me, sinking deep into my pores until I swell with the truth of my being—that I look like God and that I am loved by God. And that nothing or no one can ever change that.

It reminds me of an article I wrote for *Christianity Today*.

I am preaching to myself when I say Black is beautiful—that Black is brilliant and bold, and that books written by Black men and Black women matter. . . . We are prized people of God, stamped with imago Dei and standing with pen in hand to pour out plot and poetry and prayers with unbridled power, perspective, and personality. Slavery and suffering did not forge and force this out of us. It was there all the time—given and gifted by God with all his unconditional compassion and creativity.[4]

Maybe you need that same smoothing out too? Maybe you need the reminder that God has formed and is still forming you? That you really do look like God, and are loved by him too.

Look beyond the skin of your body.

Look beyond the color of your eyes. Look beyond the texture, length, or even the loss of your hair. Look beyond your best and worst features, your best and worst days.

Look into the loving eyes of God.

Let his gaze affirm the art that you are.

Prayer

God, thank you that I can trust your hands and your heart. You call me your beloved and you say that I belong. Help my heart to hear this truth when I look in the mirror. Help my eyes to see you even when I don't sense you beholding me. Fill me with the faith to keep believing that I am your beloved. Show me that I look like you. Teach me how to love like you. Amen.

Prompts

In what ways do you feel beloved?

In what ways do you feel like a beholder?

Practices

Work with wet clay. More than perfecting your creation, learn to love the process—the smoothing, the strokes, the pressing, and the molding. Focus on the foundations of a shape or the location of its features rather than fine details. Ponder how you are both the beloved and the beholder. Ponder how God is both the artist and the audience.

Have or hire someone to create a sketch of your features. Trace each line with your eyes and map out the location of your lips, eyes, nose, cheeks, eyebrows, and chin. Speak truth to every feature, especially any features you have trouble seeing as beautiful or beloved. Keep your sketch in a prominent place and thank God for your likeness, for the way he made you and loves you.

Pieces

In defiant beauty,
She wears her coils as a crown.
Comfortable in her own skin,
Tawny and brown,
Round nose, lips full.
All that she is—beautiful!
Unique and strong. Though relentlessly tried,
Her peace and true beauty reside inside.

—Sharla Fanous

I feel like sunrises—
dark on the surface
but brimming with the potential of brilliance.
Serene in my azure,
gracious in my pinks,
playful in my oranges–
I'm a rising beauty.

I feel like sunsets—
bright on the surface,
but obscurity creeps in quietly.
Mulling in my indigo,
pensive in my reds,
brooding in my blues–
I'm a dusky enigma.

—Jazmine Lampley

Let There Be Courage

Courage starts with showing up and letting ourselves be seen.
—Brené Brown, *Daring Greatly*

The nightmare comes to me when I least expect it, waking me up in the middle of my sleep only to leave me gasping for air and crying all in the same breath.

Home.

It's the nightmare where my oldest brother lies lifeless and limp on the floor of my childhood home. His body, thin and wasting away, is surrounded by a chalk-drawn outline, and there is a man in the dream motioning for me to take a knife and kill myself. And there I am, the one who loves my brother and would do anything for him, except for this one thing, this thing where I cannot hurt myself for the sake of helping him. I cannot save his life at the cost of losing mine.

This haunting always comes with a cut and a sting, always leaves me to wonder whether it is a premonition of some sort, like a ghost appearing, showing itself as something that I can see through but never see past.

I've wondered if it is God's way of telling me that I'll someday see this vision lived out in the flesh. That someday I'll see every chilling scene of that nightmare pan out in real life, and there won't be anything I can do to stop it.

Not a thing I can do to save my brother's life.

There is a place inside every one of us, a hidden place where we tuck away our tragedies, burying them deep in the heart where we veil our vulnerability and cover the things that have no cure. And this very place where pain is present "triggers reminders, all buzzing through blood and bone, that we are fragile and finite and that we are not in control."[1]

We are fragile because we can love and lose. We are finite because we can hold the ones we love but cannot have them forever. We are not in control because we cannot fully stop this whirling world from spinning us wild and wounded.

This is the truth about my place—the place where pain shattered my soul as I watched my brother grow up and suffer with seizures. My place cradles the untold secrets of watching my brother's rattling rib cage, watching his breathless face turn red and purple and blue. My place replays the bad thoughts I learned to memorize—like thinking his seizures sounded like broken records working past the scratch over and over again.

And I know you have a place like this too. A place that is heavy because it holds on to hurt. It might be a word that someone spoke over you or a loved one you lost too soon. It might be the loneliness that's lingered long or the ache of dreams deferred or dead.

I wonder how long you've carried your pain-filled place. I wonder if you believe that hope is on the horizon or that the dawn will rise even if you've lost the will or the words to pray.

You can hope through pain.

You can *heal* through pain.

There is a particular kind of art form that extends an invitation to peer into pain, to stare straight into your very own eyes and look within. It is an art form that continues today, an art form with a beginning that dates back to ancient Egypt.[2]

It is the self-portrait, which is a representation of an artist that is drawn, painted, photographed, or sculpted *by* that artist. And, as far removed as you may feel from this art form, the truth is that it might be one that hits closest to home.

That is because this art form has been normalized and digitized by way of phones with cameras and the cultural norm of taking and publishing selfies or, in essence, self-portraits.

A portrait, by definition, is the representation of a person's likeness. A self-portrait, however, is so much more than that.

James Hall, author of *The Self-Portrait*, writes, "But the self-portrait—more so than a portrait—is primarily a product of memory and imagination."[3] Essentially, whether by intention or not, a self-portrait is an opportunity for the artist to mirror not only their outward appearance, but their inner world.

This explains why the growing popularity of self-portraits coincided with a time when mirrors also grew in prominence. Mirrors were, and still are, more than a medium to merely observe physical features. The significance and "science" of mirrors is that displaying them is a sign of both wealth *and* knowledge—of wanting to see, and therefore know, about the world, as well as wanting to see, and therefore know, about self. We stare into mirrors not only to see the reflection of our face but to seek within us the coexistence of our treasures and traumas, our wonder *and* wounds. We gaze into the mirror so as to see the presence of the things that both inspire and injure us or, as Hall puts it, our "virtues and vices."[4]

Have you ever considered the fact that when you post a photo on Instagram, you are not just sharing your face but you are sharing your soul? Every time you photograph yourself, you are not only capturing an image of yourself, but you are confessing the inside of yourself.

I wonder if you know the power of a self-portrait, of a photo taken on your phone. I wonder if you see the emotion that drips from your face. I wonder if you know that it shows whether you were overjoyed in that moment or if there was a part of you, as seen by the look in your eyes, that ached.

There is an artist who both my mom and I find irrevocably intriguing, an artist who the world has always found eerily captivating. There is nothing that quite compares to the confessional self-portraits of Frida Kahlo, a woman whose world possessed both physical and psychological pain.

A woman who took oil to masonite and, from the very provenance of pain, painted her famous self-portrait *The Broken Column*, which holds the story of her tragedy, of living life bound in bed and with steel for a spine.

This self-portrait tells the story of Frida's place of pain, as portrayed by the plethora of nails driven into her arms, neck, and breasts.[5] *The Broken Column* shows to us the subject of intense emotional and physical pain. A woman confessing her state of suffering, a woman who says, herself, that her paintings carry "the message of pain."[6]

Frida lived acquainted with pain after fighting an infection with polio that left her limp and lame. But it was her accident on a trolley—where a handrail drove through her hip—that left her lying in bed, utterly changed.

The Broken Column is not Frida's only confessional self-portrait. *The Flying Bed* depicts her miscarriage, and *The Wounded Deer* depicts her disappointment in the surgery that was supposed to save her spine. *Thinking About Death*, which shows a hole on Frida's forehead with the skull to represent death, came as the result of her ongoing battle with disease and disability.

The interesting thing about *Thinking About Death* is the subtle way in which Frida insinuates that death is not the end-all. In this self-portrait, the background is filled with lush greens, a sign of life, a sign that is also a reflection of the Mexican belief that death is really just a pathway to rebirth and life.

All of this seeps in and out of the popular self-portraits of Frida Kahlo. Confession, by way of creativity, did not come merely because Frida Kahlo was talented and skilled. It came as the result of looking at and being faced to see herself. The story goes that Frida's parents put a mirror over her bed, attaching it to the posts hanging high above her so that she could see and study herself, becoming the subject of her own paintings.

Her confession came by way of creativity.

Her creativity came by way of *courage*.

Anna Abraham writes in *The Neuroscience of Creativity* that our knowledge sometimes keeps us from knowing more. She writes that it is difficult for the human brain to deviate from what it knows so it is easiest to ritualize that which it already knows. This idea is called conceptual constraint.[7]

Conceptual constraint bids us to settle, comfortably, into what we know. What we have experienced becomes what we expect over and over and over again. The trouble with this is it, in turn, inhibits our creativity. This means that instead of trying new things, we will resort to doing the same things. We do this to avoid the hard work that comes with figuring something out and doing it for the first time.

Repetition is easier for the brain than reimagining.

Perhaps this is true of the heart too?

Perhaps repeating the same narratives and telling the same stories is easier than reimagining new ones? Perhaps we stick to the scripts we know because it is easier than teaching ourselves new thought patterns?

I wonder what this means for those of us who are ready—or want to be ready—to live beyond our places of pain. How do we imagine hope in the midst of pain? How do we envision realities different from all we already know?

To do this would take creativity; it would take the same kind of courage required to explore realms of the unknown. It would take courage to admit the fact that you do not know all there is to know. It would take creativity to imagine, to visualize, the possibility that there really could be something else on the other side of your pain.

All of this talk about conceptual constraint and reimagining reminds me of the way Dominick Cobb, the main character in the movie *Inception*, teaches Ariadne, his apprentice, to build dreams.

Inception, which just so happens to be my favorite movie, *thank you very much*, is a science fiction film in which Cobb is a skilled idea extractor and has the uncanny ability to hack into the minds of those he is hired by to "break into" and steal, or extract, ideas and secrets from them.

Cobb, in preparation for an extraction, teaches Ariadne that when building dreams she should always imagine new places.

This is crucial because in *Inception*, building a dream from memory—from what you already know—is the easiest way to lose your grasp on reality. Cobb stresses the importance of imagining new places to Ariadne, not only because getting lost to reality *could* happen, but because it *has* happened.

Cobb, as the movie goes on, hires Ariadne to build dreams because he no longer can. Haunted by the memory of losing his wife, Cobb struggles to imagine new places; he struggles to see beyond his place of pain.

I confess, *Inception* only became important to me ten years after seeing it for the first time. A movie about hacking into a person's subconscious and stealing their deepest, hidden secrets, all while building dreams within dreams and imagining things entirely new and undone before?

It sounds confusing.

It also sounds downright impossible.

Except, it's *not* impossible.

The fantastical imagery that unfolds in this movie is almost as breathtaking as it is prophetic. It sends chills up and down my spine, watching a dream-building scene and listening to the soundtrack swell while dreams explode in the background and new ones come shooting up from the ground. Ariadne successfully learns how to create dreams where she imagines new places.

As for Cobb, he successfully learns how to look beyond his pain and venture to new places in real life.[8]

The invitation is this.

You can bravely look within yourself, to all there is within. You can peer ahead to see the possibility that lay beyond the horizon of your hurts. Not as a way of pushing down the pain but as a way of pressing on through it. Not as a way of ignoring the pain but as a way to imagine new life and hope beyond it.

If ever there was an image portraying the paradox of someone in pain but also peering into the possibility to come beyond it, it would be those rusty nails driven into the outstretched hands of Jesus Christ. It would be a portrait of the "man of sorrows" hanging on a tree, suffering his love while simultaneously giving it away.

> He is despised and rejected of men; a man of sorrows, and acquainted with grief: and we hid as it were our faces from him; he was despised, and we esteemed him not. (Isa. 53:3 KJV)

Pain is, paradoxically, a birthplace of good things—of joy, hope, even life itself.

Ask the women who give birth and give way to breath. Ask the athlete who runs until muscles atrophy how pain is a part of the very process that builds strength.

It will hurt and it will be hard, retiring the habit of returning to what you know, of staring at your hidden suffering, or your secrets, or the repeat stories that you know by heart.

But this is courage, turning the direction of your gaze, turning your face to see anew, and shifting your perspective to imagine the other side of your pain.

Isn't this the heartbeat of the Christian faith?

Existing in this broken world that we've come to know and call home, all the while making room within our imagination for the hope that heaven—a place we've yet to see—really *is* on the other side of earth.

Have you thought about that? Have you ever truly considered that our belief in a new world—for a new heaven and earth—is built on our *faith* in that world and not on the *fact* that we've seen it?

This kind of creative courage is the essence of our faith and, ultimately, our hope. It is a miracle that we might peer into our places of pain, see that we are not in control, and ultimately trust that God is.

We can peer into ourselves to see every lingering question, every doubt and mystery that suspends, like stars in the cosmos of unfathomable galaxies. And we can come to find that we need not be afraid, that we need not know everything in order to know peace and calm and healing.

We need only know God and know his goodness. In that, our awe and wonder will always lead to the kind of living that is sustained by courageous curiosity. A curiosity that goes from peering into self, to peering at God and pondering the inexplicability of his healing love—and then *believing* in it too.

This is courage.

And it is a certain kind of creativity too.

It is courage that you would tilt your perspective away from pain and toward possibility. It is creativity that you would use your imagination to see something other than what has been embedded into your mind by way of living, by way of losing.

This is not a call to pretend that you don't have pain. This is not a call to cover up pain, to push it aside, or to simply push through it.

This is a call to contemplation; it is a call to confession. It is a call to stare out into the horizon of your hurts, to name those mountains in the landscape of loss.

This call to gaze inward will ultimately cause you to gaze outward and upward. You will realize that you need friends to hold you in your hurt. You will realize that you want to open the curtains and finally welcome God's light.

Peering into and then beyond our pain will not diminish the scale of our hurt; rather, it helps us bravely distinguish hurt from the hope that was always meant to be.

May courage compel us as we travel in and through our stories. May courage cultivate creativity and lead us on in the hard work of facing all that is within us.

May we release our grip on all the ways we've allowed pain to define us. May we whisper prayers, asking for grace to ground us as we name the things that grieve us.

May this newfound perspective of pain guide the plot of our stories and determine the direction of our dreams and doings.

May it bring us to healing; may it bring us to hope.

I have this friend Ashley Beaudin who writes about self-sabotage and the pain we hold against ourselves. She's a woman who teaches other women how to truth tell. How to lean into their stories and see the version of themselves in need of healing and help. She is a woman who honors the practice of paying attention. She is beautiful and profound and wise. *How's that for an introduction?*

During the COVID-19 pandemic, Ashley did·a ten-day self-portrait challenge. One of her self-portraits had her whole body submerged in water. Half her face hovers over the water while the other half is submerged, and there is a serene reflection of her face upon the water. About her self-portrait, she writes:

> I am doing this ten-day experiment of holding myself with love through self-portraits. Believe it or not, this is a selfie. As I looked at this photo, I thought about how in a season of lockdown where I've longed for the embrace of others, I've discovered that nature itself could hold me. And so I've let it. What peace I've found in this.

Her self-portrait reflected what was inside of her—a longing that lingered and, through the taking of this self-portrait, was found and realized.

Peace.

She found peace.

I wish that I could portray with my words the bliss that exudes from Ashley's self-portrait. But I cannot. It is too beautiful, too serene to possibly tell you the way that light and shadow dance upon the reflection of her face in the water.

I couldn't possibly tell you the way in which her face is poised with such peace. The tilt of her head, a delicate turning of a confident and courageous chin upward.

This kind of courage can be yours too. This kind of looking inward to then look outward and upward—in peace—is an invitation for you too.

And there is no pressure to be professional. You do not need to take yearlong courses, do not need to pursue photography as a career or even a craft to commit to.

You need only courage, daring audacity to look long into every corner and crevice of your heart. You need only to be willing to authentically unearth that which is within—whether it be a place of pain or even just a place of pensive pondering. You might even be surprised to look within yourself and see joy or peace.

After peering comes the self-portrait. It can be a painting; it can be a sketch; it can be watercolor spread thin on canvas, or a photo taken by phone or camera. Self-portraits can be created again and again, coming out of different seasons and for different reasons.

You need only to believe that you can behold yourself.

You need only to believe that you see the beauty that is all around.

You need only to believe in the gaze of a God who calls you good—need only to trust in his call for you to live with courage, to trust his heart.

To trust his healing hand.

Prayer

God, peer into my places where pain is present. Cultivate courage in my heart and remind me that my story is safe with you. Surround me with people who will help me see what I need and who I am. Call me deeper into your truth, call me higher into healing. Help me cradle the courage to create from the truth of where I am. Help me cradle the courage to believe in where your love can take me. Amen.

Prompts

Look at a self-portrait or selfie, what pain do you see?

Look at a self-portrait or selfie, what peace do you see?

Practices

Create a self-portrait. Take or draw a picture of yourself. Pick an outfit that you feel comfortable and confident in. Wear your hair and makeup the way you normally do or try a style that you've been wanting to try. Include props that have special meaning or can serve as representations of values and beliefs you hold deeply and dearly.

Print and/or edit your self-portrait. Part of what makes a self-portrait so special is that it is the artist's own interpretation of themself. Write words across your face, scribble out body parts, add sketches to emphasize elements that mean something to you. Research the self-portraits of your favorite artists. Practice the strokes and styles that you see and make them your own.

Pieces

Perhaps God doesn't send billowing smoke clouds,
    words on open,
High-ceilinged walls to heal a brain, a heart, a body.
Maybe the enchanting
Thing about such a mystical, yet solid faith is that healing comes where we
Want it least. Where we let failure, grace, and an
    unexpected place see
Who we are—but not leave us as we are.

—Peyton Garland

I'll meet you in that place
between there and here.
I'll tell you it's okay to
honor
your story.
Not the one created for you by them,
but the one created for you by Him.
I'll wrap you in a hug
and tell you that it's ok to
honor
your feelings
all of them
the imperfect ones especially.
I'll gather your fears and your tears and
honor
that they are a part of who you were,
and pave the way for who you will become.
I'll
honor
you, and in that
you will finally
honor
you, too.

                       —Katie Drobina

5

Let There Be Home

Place is always present in a poem.

—Joy Harjo, *The Field of Stories*

If I tell you that I am typing with smolder on my hands and watching a rising fire under the burn of wood and wind . . .

If I tell you that my view is not of a window or of the walls within my house, but that I am looking up at the southern pines standing tall like soldiers, and that the sky is fading from the brightest blue to the dimmest dark . . .

If I tell you that just last night "I heard the small kingdoms breathing around me, the insects, and the birds who do their work in the darkness,"[1] and that I slept to the sound of cicadas calling out to one another, calling out to me . . .

Would you be able to guess where I am?

Do you taste the dampened air of the forest; do you feel the fog setting in, the heat of the sun lifting over? Do you hear sound and sense where I am? Do you see and can you tell how place prompts poetry, both the witness and the writing of it?

A cabin in the woods.

That is where I am, and there is poetry in the pillar of the trees, in the heart of this place, and it is both a practice and a profession of faith to dare to still your soul to see all that surrounds, to perceive it all as a poetic performance.

And, what's more, it's poetry to pen these things down.

Poetry and place. They are two words that go together, like salt and pepper, day and night, up and down, and high and low. The two go together and they cannot be separated, and if you do not know this, then you are forfeiting a certain kind of attention, a certain kind of appreciation that lends way to art.

Poetry finds its grounding in place, finds its beginning in the bones of witness, and finds its rhythm in watching that which swells within and all around.

I *could* have told you that I was writing these words from a picnic table outside of a cabin, but without color and texture and sound, there is no poem, no portal for you to travel through to see and sense it all for yourself.

Your home is not a humdrum of mundanity. Your home is a holding place of magic. And with the surrounding scenery of dishes that swell and the tasks that mound like laundry piles, like mountains of weight that crush your craving for creativity, I know that you must be asking yourself, *How do I find poetry in the everyday?*

You must be wondering what could possibly be beautiful about the broken shades that cover your window, the handprints smeared across your front door. You must be wondering how on earth you can hear beauty in the midst of the spinning dryer, the tossing dishwasher, the kids screaming, and the TV blaring. How do you find the extraordinary in the ordinary? How do you find something worth writing about, something worth creating?

How do you use these ordinary moments as your color palette from which to paint or create?

Easy.

Listen to the sounds of your location. This is an act that requires stillness, that requires attention.

This is an act that is less about getting found and more about getting lost. Getting lost in the details of where you are and what you are doing and, most importantly, who you are with.

People think that a poem must always be about feelings. This is why so many shy away from poetry, why they say that they could never write a poem, could never be a poet.

I used to think the same thing when I was a college student taking creative writing classes. In one of my classes, we were instructed to keep a journal, one that we should fill with our own thoughts and musings. I took composition notebooks and colored over them to make them my own.

The paper was blank, my pen was ready. I had everything I needed to begin.

After a few weeks of writing in my journal, my professor left a note on the page of one of my entries. I had been wandering on and on, writing about my own inner world, penning down my own observations of self, self, and self.

The professor wrote and challenged that, maybe, it would suffice to write about the world around me. To write beyond my observations of self, self, and self.

Offense was the first feeling. Then embarrassment. Then pride. I didn't want him to read my words anymore. He didn't value or validate my feelings, it seemed.

But it wasn't until years later, years after I'd graduated, that I realized the value of this feedback, the value of deviating from my own view to a worldview. A practice that, essentially, has more to do with being grounded in places with people than it does with poetry.

And so, I'm eager to know.

What is your place and who are your people? What is the color of your walls, the weight of your doors? How many stains are in your carpet, or are they hardwood floors? And in your cupboard do the mugs match or are they all one of a kind?

Are there photos on your walls?

Do vines creep up your trellis?

Do you come from a city that is busy with buses?

Were you raised on a farm?

The moments and minutes of your life, the descriptions and details, this is the stuff of your making, your creating. The material from which you will draw. Poetry, really, is dwelling. And it can be a home for you. It can be a home to hold you. It can house you with warmth when you are cold, and the walls can mirror that which is within you.

> Still—
> and when you finally do hush rampant thoughts
>   running fast and wild and free,
> so that the only hum around you is the syncopated
>   song of whispering clocks,
> or tumbling heat turning round the gathered piles to
>   breathe them dry,

or the fan pushing air through slits on walls in high
    places,—then, you will feel the warm of morning's
    sun transcending,
transpiring,
through windows that welcome light like open doors.
Then, you will see its glistening color paint the world,
that sparkle on the green leaf,
bodies of illuminated effervescence passing like ships
    as sea.
Then, you will feel cold,
or heat,
or whatever kind of air you wake and sleep in,
wrap around your hollow bones.
And you will feel it, the chill or the heat of it, and
    you will know exactly where you are—the moment
    seeping itself into your senses.
You will stand,
or sit,
or spin in incandescent rapture.
And you will know exactly where you are—and, in
    momentary brevity,
know exactly who you are.

There is a God out there, and he is not a god of generality but of particularity. He is concerned with distilling details, with the way they dance across the landscape of our lives.

And if we can learn to look at things the way God does, we can learn to *see* the way he does. This can become a practice in which penning the particular of your days becomes a pathway to seeing the beauty in them—not just another load of clothes to wash, but textiles that hold the scent of your newborn baby. Not just papers on your desk but data with names and numbers—papers that document the life of the clients you serve.

In the middle of COVID-19, when the world seemed to be getting back to normal, I ventured out to my first public event. Masked, I made my way to the Blumenthal Performing Arts Center in uptown Charlotte where the streets turn and twist so much they even confuse the natives.

I was there to participate in a poetry project that started in New Zealand and made its way over here to Charlotte, North Carolina.

We were to spend our time writing to a certain set of prompts. Our facilitator introduced himself then introduced the theme. *The center of the world.*

"The center of the world" is a line that comes from Joy Harjo's poem "My House is the Red Earth," in which she talks about the land as being the center of her world.[2] She hones in on a particular place, a place nameless and unknown to countless others. But to her it is everything. To her, home is hinged upon this place.

So, there I am, writing to this prompt, *the center of the world*, and then we are given more prompts to get closer and closer to detailing and naming the specifics of the place we are writing about.

I decide that I do not want to write about an emotional place like I often do.

I decide that I want to write about the exterior world—what is happening around me and what I see.

I write about the lake near my house, the place I've called home for the past four years. The first lines of my poem offer directions, welcoming others to come to my place, to the center of my world.

I'll tell you how to get there, how to—
take that stretch of road from Uptown to up north.

How to—
drive twenty-five
minutes and miles

to the place where water whispers,
the place where waves wrap 'round some fifty-four
     miles of small-town charm.

The first line of my poem speaks to the truth that poetry is not only a place for yourself but it is a place offered up to others. Poetry welcomes others to find themselves in your words. It welcomes them to see themselves in your setting.

In that, others find a sense of safety, a sense of sureness, and a sense of security. Through words that drip with exactness and details, poetry gives proof that another person walks a shared path with you.

Isn't this the greatest way of serving our neighbors, of saying *me too*?

Poetry reminds us that we are not alone, that we have never been alone, and that we will never be alone. It offers a sort of communion, a kind space to share with someone. It is a humble form of hospitality, of swinging wide open the door of your soul, as if to say the things that confess that state of your soul.

It is an invitation.

It is a welcome.

It is home.

I want to tell you that you do not have to feel alone, that you are, in fact, not alone.

I want to tell you that there just might be another who understands the sound of floorboards creaking under the weight of feet. There is another soul somewhere out there in the world who understands couches covered in crumbs, sticky floors, and gardens growing wild with weeds.

Your home, your work, your backyard, your office—these places that seem mundane are actually filled with *so* much.

You really are surrounded by the stuff that magic is made of.

You really are surrounded by people and places worthy to be penned in poems.

The rug beneath your feet.

The sunken couch where your father lays.

The empty room.

The fridge of familiar faces.

The shelf with curry and cumin.

The *kimchi* on the counter.

All of these things punctuate your life with color, sense, sound, and texture. All of these things offer themselves to you—as first lines, as stanzas, as couplets in poems.

And for the times when you do not wish to write poems, for the people who do not ever wish to write poems, so be it. But then, at least, *taste* poetry.

Make space in your life for the frequent reading of poetry. Keep books of poems on your nightstand, in the car, and by the couch: Rupi Kaur, Emily Dickinson, Amanda Gorman, John Keats, Langston Hughes, Joy Harjo, Shel Silverstein, Mary Oliver, T. S. Eliot.

Read poems because they will teach you to tarry. They will show you how to slow down to see the gold in the hair of your child, all the creeping vines on your house. Poetry will teach you how to consider the story of that table in your dining room—to think about the swirl in the wood grain and who the table once belonged to.

Poetry will teach you to slow down and see the smiling faces on your fridge. It will teach you to buy more flowers, to buy more paintings, to breathe fresh air.

You will begin to see your home, or whatever space that holds you, as holy. You will begin to be content with where you are. You will practice blessing the place of your belonging, giving thanks, living with love.

Someday you will move into the house of your dreams. Someday you will travel to exotic cities and countries. Someday you will prepare exquisite meals in pristine places. Someday you will wake to clean kitchens and bathrooms.

Someday.

For now, though, let the LEGOs litter your living room. Let bills pile up and mail move from one dusty table to the next. Live for the moments, because someday they will become memories. Someday, when you move away from your place, it will become an ache.

The kids will grow, the house will sell, and the state on the license plate will change.

But if you let it, *a poem* can preserve the details of your place. When landscapes change and memories dwindle, it will be poems, like this one by Elizabeth Mowers of Fallow Ink, that echo on with life and love.

> There is scarcely a memory of yours,
> separate from mine. The shape of your
>
> days, for better or worse, formed by
> my words, my choices, my thoughts,

though they always reach to enfold.
Your learning, your discovery, served

to you with my hands. But now
there is that first flutter of separate lives.

There. Just below my rib cage. I press
my hand, searching for the shift—sometimes

sharp, and sometimes just a slight hollow
feeling. You have whole hours and days now,

that stretch without my face in your view.
Experiences, conversations and new pieces

of information obtained without my ever knowing.
I rejoice in your expanding universe, bask in

the radiance of the world at your grasping,
still-chubby hands. I delight to watch you go

marching up mountains of all sizes, made of
whimsy and imagination. It's just . . . this small ache

at my side—just here, below my rib cage—
where I'll rest my hand, as I watch you climb.

These words bring to me memories of my own kids, of moments watching them reach for toys and run through the rooms of our too-small home. This poem, it transports me, makes me travel in time.

Poems can transport you too. They can take you home or to that mountain you once saw or to the road trip driving your dad's Volvo across state lines.

There are no details too small, too minute, too mundane. And there is no place too plain to be penned in a poem.

Even if that poem is only enjoyed by you.

Prayer

God, tune my ears to hear the song of my creaking floor-boards. Turn my eyes to see the sunken couch as a sacred holding of belonging souls. Soften my lips to bless the walls in my place of dwelling. Help me appreciate the place and people of my home. Help me to see that it houses meaning, wild hope, and creativity. Amen.

Prompts

Where is the place of your home?
Who are the people of your home?

Practices

Write a poem about your home. Home, as in where you are from or where you are now. Paint a picture with your words. Show the colors of the shutters, the size of the doorframe, and what the doorbell sounds like. Show us the greenery: Are there trees or flower bushes? Are there neighboring houses? Does it sit on a hill? Are there cows in the distance? Is it drowned in the sight of skyscrapers and the sound of cars whizzing by?

It's time to put your own words on the walls. Pause from purchasing decor from department stores and instead print and display a piece that you've written about your own home. You can print it on paper then place it in a frame, or you can print it on canvas. You can write or paint the words straight onto the walls if you dare. Use what you have or get what you need to make what you've always wanted. If you are someone who moves a lot, be sure to display your poem or piece in a way that can easily be transported.

Pieces

Search for the glimmer, when Divinity interrupts ordinary.
It's easy to fancy the extraordinary life, and forget that
    the Divine came born ordinary.
Walked ordinary.
Lived ordinary.
The people who were healed, oftentimes they seemed to
    be ordinary people.
The disciples, too.
Yet, our Savior met them just the same.
Be wary of the one(s) who push dreams of
    extraordinary,
who beckon you to lust for more.
Seek the quiet voice, the soft whisper,
look for glimmers of Presence—the Divine Presence of
    God who seems to love showing up in the ordinary.
Oh ordinary. You truly are a gift.
May we all embrace you so.

—Alexa Mason

We have not thrived.
We have slid into home all banged up and bruised every
    single night.
We have screamed, cried, and thrown royal fits.
Every one of us.

My house is in disarray. My mind is spinning with to-do's.
My hands are full of beauty and pain because the real
messes inside are oozing out.
Holding today's pain and tomorrow's hope is hard.
But every day we show up—inching closer to rock
bottom.
Yes, it's a mess, inside and out, but there's a special
presence in the mess. One that cradles with tender
love and deep truths—showing up with us and
washing the shame and failure from our daily slate.

It's a beautiful thing. A glorious presence.
Never wanting us to fabricate perfection and happiness.
Always wanting us to bring authentic imperfection and
sorrow.

So bring it all to the table. Lighten your load. Eat cereal
for dinner. Laugh a little bit. Cry a lot. Show up.
Because for everything there is a time . . . And He
will keep you through all of it.

—Sarah Koch

6

Let There Be Play

Invitations to play are all around. Kids are experts at spotting them. We can learn again.

—Courtney Ellis, *Happy Now*

I mentioned in an earlier chapter that my favorite movie is *Inception*, but I did not bend and twist my words to tell you about Dominick Cobb, and how he is one of my favorite fictional characters. I did not tell you about the times I sit alone in my car listening to the soundtrack of *Inception*, playing the song "Time" on repeat, letting it loop so much I lose count.

Alone in my car.

I didn't tell you how "Time" swells with wonder and weight, how I cry and mourn to this song, how I slice sausage and openly weep in the kitchen to this song. I didn't tell you how the song makes me feel all kinds of small as I wonder about life and human existence. As I mourn and grieve my losses, counting and naming them one by one—the lives lost to COVID-19, the fading friendships, the breakage in my body.

I know I am not the only one in the world who feels this way. I know I am not the only one who has been touched deeply by this song and its musical arrangement of notes played on the piano. I know I am not the only one, because on YouTube I see comments like confessions, saying it's the most beautiful song and how it feels like the soundtrack of the universe.

I play the song on my phone. I check out the album from the library. I read the sheet music of it on Google. I play it on YouTube, repeating it one thousand and one times.

One day, I forget to rewind the song and YouTube, on autoplay, went to the next video which was a live recording of "Time" at Hollywood in Vienna in 2018 for The World of Hans Zimmer tour.[1] As I write this, the video has been streamed 15,978,540 times since November 23, 2018—the day the video was published.

I am drawn into the video, watching stage lights ricochet off of shiny brass instruments. The conductor waves his hands in the air, and chandeliers illuminate the ceiling above a captivated audience. Shadows on the wall shape-shift to mirror the hands of the musicians they mimic—the drummer, the cellists, the flutists, the violinists.

Then comes the sound of an electric guitar, and a man with silver hair emerges from the side of the stage. It is Hans Zimmer, and the look on his face is nothing like that which I'd imagined it to be. It is not a look of depth, or contemplation, or grave solemnity. Rather, it is a look of sheer pleasure.

I am surprised at what I see, because either my eyes are mistaking me, or Hans Zimmer is as happy as he appears to be. Curiosity compels me, so much so that I take the deepest dive into videos of interviews with Hans Zimmer. I'm desperate to know more about this man—what compels him to compose songs that string notes of sorrow yet smile while playing them.

Then, I find it. The reason for the smile behind his playing. As the camera pans around the burning candles in his studio, with mixers stretched long against the walls, he says:

> The most important word about music is the word "play." It's like kids sitting there with LEGOs. It always is. When music sounds good it's because it's playing. You have to have a playfulness if you do these situations. It gives you an opportunity to show off the music and what is good about humanity.[2]

I stop the YouTube video and rewind it, again and again, until his words sink in. Until I am sure that I am understanding every syllable he has uttered—playing music is not all performance and perfection. It is about pleasure, he says. It is about having fun.

I'm reminded of my husband—a skilled guitarist, violinist, drummer, all-around musician—who knows and practices music theory, harmonics, pitch, and scales. He often comes home at night simply wanting to play his guitar because it's "fun."

Childhood memories flash before my mind of my dad in his music room playing bass just because he wanted to. Memories of myself also come flooding in, reminding me of the pleasure and passion I feel when I play progressions of chords on the piano or sing songs that take me in and out of time, in and out of body, in and out of every emotion.

Hans Zimmer is right.

Music is, and will always be, *play.*

The thing about play is that we've come to believe that we cannot grow up and still possess our childlike wonder. We've come to believe that we live only for our obligations and therefore shouldn't waste time in entertaining our imaginations.

Who is it that decides that the child within cannot grow and go with us? How do we release ourselves from the lie? How do we enchant ourselves to return to belief in the breath of dragons, the flickering wings of fairies, the color in crayons, the leisure of LEGOs?

Here's the secret.

We see not by sight, but by saying *yes*.

The truth is that play is a choice—an intentional pursuit. It is something we set out in search of, something we find only when we first find our souls in humble submission. It is something we say *yes* to, even amid life's demands and time constraints.

"Playfulness," says Courtney Ellis, "begins with a first, simple yes." She writes:

> We are often far too focused on completing the necessary tasks of life to spend time pursuing frivolity. Put another way, who has time to play when the challenges facing us are so very, very serious? As Thomas Hobbes famously wrote, life can be "solitary, poor, nasty, brutish, and short." Scripture describes our lives as fading as quickly as "the flowers of the field" (1 Pet. 1:24). We don't have much time here on this earth, and the time we do have overflows with obstacles, tedium, and heartache. The paradox of play is this: We engage in whimsy not because life is easy but because life is difficult.[3]

We can engage in whimsy. We can enchant ourselves to amusement once again. We can look around at our beckoning lives and instead hear and heed the call to pause and wonder, to laugh and let go. We can learn to be okay with finding ourselves in seasons, even seconds, of singing with silliness or playful improvising.

It is not a waste of time to pretend you can fly, to dance undignified, or to color outside the lines. On the contrary, play is important. Play is practice for real life—it expands the mind to think, dream, solve, and imagine.

We need play for fun. But we also need play to *become*. It is formative and transformative. We believe this for kids. Can we believe it for ourselves?

I will never forget my time at Nyack College when I launched and led a small group that I called The Playpen. Before the semester began, I sat inside the Betty Knopp House on campus, surrounded by all the other small group leaders. The professor asked each of us to share our plans for leading our small groups.

I shared the idea that I had in my mind—the vision of our chapel hall filled with seeking students coming to color with crayons, listening to children's stories, lounging on floors, and finding reprieve. What I envisioned, and what eventually did come to pass, was a room full of stressed students wanting to be kids again, wanting to be free from obligation, if only for an hour once a week.

I didn't want another small group filled with Bible studies, hour-long prayer meetings, or deep conversations about trying harder in our academics and athletics. What I wanted, and what I imagined everyone wanted, was a safe place to unravel and unwind.

A place for *being* and not for *doing*.

In the small group leader meeting, I exhale these words as the idea cascades out of me like a confession on trembling lips.

A hush falls over the room, falls deep into my heart. There is silence—a long and awkward pause. The professor looks at me and, with eyes staring into mine, he says:

Don't confuse being childlike with being childish.

Gears move and shift deep within the core of my heart. And now everything makes sense. Everything is illuminated and light begins to shine bright on the seed taking root in my heart. A truth was spoken. A truth had been planted in a place that once cradled a lie.

Don't confuse being childlike with being childish.

As in, don't confuse being imaginative with being immature. Don't believe that it is bad or wrong or silly to live *and* lead from a place of play, a place of wild imagination. Don't believe that you do not need play or pleasure.

Don't believe that it is not cathartic.

Don't believe that it is not creative.

We can learn to play once again by paying attention, by looking to the places within our hearts that hold the memories and moments we found fascinating as a child. We learn to play by returning to the things that once brought us sheer pleasure— the collection of cars, bedtime stories, cutting cookies on the counter, staring up into the sky to count an endless display of stars.

We can learn again to live creatively and artfully by looking to the things that give us breath and take our breath away. In the here and now, right in the middle of our living. With tools as toys and gadgets as games.

It starts by saying yes to the thrills that intrigue and enchant you.

It starts by embracing your imagination to color the black and white of your world.

Like a child scribbling color from crayons with no regard for rules, no care for the concept of compartmentalized boxes, play ushers in freedom, a kind of a curious exploration.

It looks like Lucy Pevensie in *The Lion, the Witch and the Wardrobe* turning the knob and walking into the hidden world of Narnia.[4] Cradling a playful perspective, Lucy welcomed possibility, a grand allowance for the existence of things outside of the ordinary.

Might it be that the same can be true for us? Might we also be able to cradle a playful perspective? Might we also be willing to place curious palms on knobs of doors or poke and prod our way through crowded coat closets?

This matter of play is more about truth than it is about time. It's just as much about belief in purpose as it is about belief of pleasure. It matters to do things because you want to and not because you have to. It matters to believe that you exist not simply because of what you can do but because of who you are.

It matters to live knowing that you can pause in the middle of all that presses and choose to play your piano for the simple fact that you like the way it sounds. It matters to pick up the garden shears, not simply because the weeds need tending but because your mind needs mindless meandering, needs a way to see beauty, to know levity.

It matters to tell stories as a way of shaving off sorrow, as a way of instilling hope into the minds of the children you teach or foster or raise. It matters for every executive, entrepreneur, pastor, and parent to live a life of play. It matters because the impact of play can extend beyond personal benefit. Living a life of creative play can go on to inspire and influence classrooms, communities, churches, and children.

This ripple effect reminds me of the story of one particular woman—a grieving, penniless widow and homeschooling mother—whose cultivation of play was one of the most formative elements in the life of her son.

She welcomed her son to step into a world of wonder by way of play. She cultivated curiosity and creative learning by teaching an appreciation for calligraphy, classic literature, and tales about dragons. Captivated by such wonder, her son eventually went on to create his own fairy stories, writing books about beasts and fantastical beings like dwarves, wizards, orcs, and elves.[5]

Though the son lost his mother at a very young age, "her labors, however," writes Jon Miltimore, "kindled the mind of a child; and that mind would go on to inspire millions more, and create a world of unparalleled beauty and imagination."[6]

That child was J. R. R. Tolkien.

And his awe-inspiring stories still rest on the lists of bestselling books worldwide.

Prayer

God, invite me into play again. Help me trust that there is more than enough time. Teach me to let my heart run wild. Open my eyes to see the world as a playground. Open my heart to see my home as a playroom. Soften my expectations. Instill a childlikeness to embrace and extend invitations for smiling, coloring, creating, playing, and laughing. Amen.

Prompts

What did play look like as a kid?
What does play look like now?

Practices

Think back to childhood and ponder a playful pastime you had as a kid. This can be anything: chalk art, lanyard, string beads, Jenga blocks, board games, hide-and-seek around the neighborhood, nature explorations, paint on easels, music on tin cans, anything. Share a memory or two of this experience with your kids, a spouse, a friend, a sibling, or an aging parent.

Join a recreation group to explore a playful practice that has nothing to do with performance: art lessons, photography classes, local foraging groups, travel abroad trips, museum memberships, *anything.*

Pieces

Kids remind me that the world is new even when it seems old. Peanut butter and jelly sandwiches become fuel for pirates and archeologists when eaten out of a plastic baggie in the backyard, the sun rises every day but we have to get up and see it today, this very moment, because "Look, Mom! The sky is pink!"

I get called to watch sprinklers, hawks, the delivery truck, chipmunks and a thousand other daily miracles, to pause in my pursuit of boring grown-up to-dos and engage in wonder.

—Dani Nichols

I am untelling
the lie
that says
creativity is only for the creatures that have

bested the beast of busyness.

I am unchecking
the box
that reads
"accomplish all tasks
to earn your right to write, your right to rest."

I am untripping
the guilt
that leaches onto my heart
that removes the 'cans,'
and replaces them with 'shoulds'
of someone else's choosing,
rendering my mind
resentful and resistant
to the joy all around me,

the possibilities prodding me,
the opportunities opening up before me.

I am writing
beside
the toy-scattered floor.
I am writing
among
the overflowing loads of laundry.
I am writing
over
the dirty dishes that pile and plead for attention.

I am filling my pages
with works of wonder
without plan or purpose or profit, but only playfulness
    and peace.

—Emily Pukuma

7

Let There Be Fairy Tales

Fairy tales are more than true: not because they tell us that dragons exist, but because they tell us that dragons can be beaten.

—Neil Gaiman, *Coraline*

It was not a church service that soothed my soul; it was a story, scenes from the script of a movie about robot aliens in a fight between good and evil.

Nyack College.

I remember where I was, my broken and unbelieving self, sitting in a dorm room surrounded by silent hallways and hollowed spaces—the telltale sign of the end of yet another school year.

I'm sitting there, eyes staring at the screen, watching Sam Witwicky as played by Shia LaBeouf in *Transformers*.

Charged with a task that could save the world, Sam runs to escape the grip of Megatron, the leader of the evil Decepticons. He climbs to the top of a skyscraper while holding the All Spark cube, from which all life is centered. Afraid to look down, he shuffles along the edge of the building, breath trembling. Then, Megatron speaks in a voice that booms with darkness and evil.

"Is it fear or courage that compels you, fleshling?" he asks Sam.

Flustered and afraid, Sam whispers under his breath, "Where do I go?"

This is just seconds before he falls from the top of the now shattering skyscraper. Descending in free fall, Sam's body turns and spins until he is rescued by the hand of Optimus Prime—rescued by an alien robot.

"I got you, boy," says Optimus Prime, and they drop from the sky together, Prime's body breaking the fall.[1]

As I watched this fictional moment of reckoning, of Sam facing his fears and bracing himself through failure, I realized that I, too, wanted to land without wreckage.

In my undergraduate years when I often felt lost and misguided, I wanted so desperately for God to catch and cradle me. As I struggled to understand whether I was, like Sam, compelled by fear or courage, I wanted nothing more than to hear God say, *I've got you, child. I've got you.*

I wanted God to break the fall of my cascading doubt.

This question of being compelled by fear or courage was not a question posed solely for Sam Witwicky. It was for me and *is* for you. It is for every person who feels afraid and unsure about God, about life, about faith, about purpose.

And isn't it poignant, so powerful, that a movie can do this—that fiction can do this? This is why stories, why the creative arts, are important and necessary.

Because fictional stories, in all their forms—from novels to movies to musicals to story-driven video games—tell us tales that tell us truth. Just as L'Engle writes: "It is not that 'God' is a myth, but that myth is the revelation of a divine life in man."[2]

————

That which is imagined has the propensity to reveal to and remind us of that which is true. We *know* when we are watching *The Wizard of Oz* that there is no such thing as a talking lion. Yet the Cowardly Lion was created not to tell us that lions talk in real life, but to tell us that fear can be overcome by even the most unassuming of characters.[3]

We *know* that the point of *Beauty and the Beast* isn't to tell us that beasts are real or that chinaware can talk under a spell in a tale as old as time. The point of *Beauty and the Beast* isn't to persuade us to believe in enchanted castles; rather, it is the reinvented telling of a timeless truth—that we can look beyond the appearance of things. That we can love someone beyond what they look like, even beyond what they've done.[4]

The real magic of *Beauty and the Beast* is that it tells us to believe in the very truths that are foundational to the Christian faith—that nothing is irredeemable, that no person is unlovable.

This is why we need comics like *X-Men* that tell stories about society's strangest outcasts. We need to be told that our weaknesses can be seen as strengths to help the world. We need characters like Storm to show us how women can live and lead, no matter the weaknesses, wounds, or ways of their past.[5]

We need TV series like *The Walking Dead* showing us that life and light can shine in the midst of death and darkness. We need the Ricks, Glenns, Daryls, and Carols to remind us of our humanity—the inevitability of loss and our capacity to love, even still.[6]

We need stories like *Jingle Jangle* reminding us that it's never too late to begin again. It's never too late to live from a place of childlike wonder, a world spinning wild with curiosity and creativity.[7]

We need scenes like the one from *Harry Potter* when the professors are standing around Hogwarts, pushing back dementors, pushing back the darkness with defiant faith and sacrificial love.[8]

We need movies like *Toy Story* to show us how to survive through the changes of life, the seasons in which we fall in and out of relationships with the ones we love and the ones who love us.[9]

We need characters like Lucy the Valiant in *The Chronicles of Narnia*.[10] Lucy, being the youngest and the first of four children to believe in Narnia, demonstrates the truth that God is always in the habit of choosing "the weak things of the world to confound the things which are mighty" (1 Cor. 1:27 KJV).

We always need characters like Deloris Van Cartier, or Sister Mary Clarence, from *Sister Act* who lives life on the run only to find forgiveness and friendship in the last place she'd expect.[11]

We need characters like Silas Marner to remind us that love can come even after life's losses.[12] We need characters like Frodo Baggins to show us we can't carry the weight of the world alone and characters like Samwise Gamgee to shoulder the burden when we try.[13]

We need the Anne Shirleys[14] and Jo Marches[15] who remind us of all the bravery and brashness, the imagination and intelligence, the wit and warmth that we know to be true of ourselves.

We need fictional places like the East African country of Wakanda to help us imagine how wealthy kingdoms can wield power for good.[16]

We need the Gollums who show us depravation and where our insatiable tendencies will take us if we surrender to them.[17]

We need all the epics, folklore, mythology, and worldview literature. We need all the comic books, cartoons, movies, plays, and novellas. We need all the fiction because it helps reveal the truth about God.

Fiction makes God easy to be sensed.

Fiction makes God easy to be seen.

And we do not have to fear fiction; we don't have to fear that it will teach us to believe in what is not true. We don't have to hesitate to enjoy what has been conjured up and created by others.

We can listen to folklore and watch movies. We can crack open our books of fiction, as much as we crack open the beloved Bible. We can partake in the art of others without worrying if it will lead us astray.

Fiction is a faithful way of learning.

Fiction is a faithful way of *loving*.

I cannot tell you why you should read or watch *Harry Potter* for yourself. I cannot tell you the ways in which it might enrich your life, your faith. What I can tell you, though, is why you will, for the rest of your life, brush shoulders with people—in stores, and schools, and stadiums—who have tattoos of the word "Always" scripted across their wrists.

What I *can* tell you is that any time you see someone with this tattoo, you can know that they have been touched; they have been irrevocably moved by Severus Snape and his selfless, sacrificial love—the kind that gave his life for the sake of saving others.[18]

This is why movie theaters will always hush gathered hearts by the millions. This is why crowds of people will always sit before widescreens. They enjoy the thrill of watching their favorite characters live out the kind of love and loyalty they wish for themselves. It's because stories touch us deep inside, telling us what we hope for and want to believe in.

It isn't futile and it isn't fruitless to be fascinated with fiction in the way that you are. It isn't weird and it isn't a waste of time to fall in love with the characters in books you read or the shows you watch. These characters are teaching you something about loss, about love. They are teaching you something about living in light and pushing back the dark.

And you do not need to fear the supernatural—the superhuman, the superheroes, even the spells or curses bound within mythical, literary worlds. In fact, it just might be that these elements can and should be echoes and whispers of the very truth that we, *ourselves*, are a people who possess supernatural abilities.

We believe in and engage with a God who encompasses mysteries and performs miracles. We pray for mountains to be moved, and we partake in the work of making it happen. We celebrate the resurrection of a Savior raised from death to life.

Our faith is hinged upon impossibilities made possible. Fiction, if we let it, can help remind our hearts to believe that.

"To be authentically Christian is to be supernatural," says Lawrence Yuen. "For us to deny this dimension of our faith makes us more like the Muggles in Harry Potter—barely worth a mention in the grand story and impotent before the *real* powers of darkness at work in our midst."[19]

The more you know this, the more you will find freedom in exploring fiction. Not merely the reading and watching of it, but also the writing of it. It is one thing to enjoy the stories of another. It is another thing to enjoy creating stories yourself.

Your stories—the ideas and characters that you create, the conflicts that you conjure up to rise and swell on the pages of your short stories and indie scripts—will awaken your eyes to see beyond what *is* into what *could be.*

Writing fiction is a brave way of believing; it is a most daring way to foster the dream of a crumbling world being saved by characters in conflict—characters in crisis, in courage, in constant development. Characters whose journeys mirror our own.

We are characters of our own, always growing and changing, as the story of our lives reads on. We are works of art becoming—page by page, breath by breath. We are turning pages toward good endings. We are fostering redemption. At least, that's what we hope for.

Your stories and scripts, your poems and plays—these are all pieces of work, *yes.* But they are also worship. In the same way that God created the world, you—through your penning and plotting—are creating too.

You are creating stories and you are creating worlds. As you do this, you bear witness to the creativity of God. Such power, such purpose, such pleasure, such praise. By writing your stories, you are giving *him* glory. David C. Downing writes of this concerning Tolkien:

> As a Christian, Tolkien could view sub-creation as a form of worship, a way for creatures to express the divine image in them by becoming creators. As a fantasy writer, Tolkien could affirm his chosen genre as one of the purest of all fictional modes, because it called for the creation not only of characters and incidents, but also of worlds for them to exist.[20]

I have learned and am learning from Tolkien's theory of sub-creation that we can be awed by a storyteller's creativity *just as much as* we can be awed by their created stories. It's because, when it comes to writing fiction, we are not simply creating story—a sequence of events taking place, one after another. Like God, we are building whole worlds into existence. We are establishing laws, languages, and landscapes. We are setting forces into motion; we are breathing life into lungs.

Your creativity is cosmic, even when it goes unseen by the world.

Will you still tell these stories, even when they are not bound in spines and sold in bookstores? Will you still create characters, even though their purpose is unclear and their ending unsure? Will you still outline the vision in your head, even though the world may never see, read, or need it?

Will you still write the stories?

Even if they are only for you?

There is a reason why the purchasing and playing of video games rose in 2020, going from 214 million to 227 million—up by 13 million in just one year.[21] It's because video games are not just video games. They are stories with whole worlds, stories with characters going from conflict to courage.

Ask any millennial who played *The Legend of Zelda: Ocarina of Time*.[22] Ask your teenager, the one who sits at the screen for hours without end talking through their wireless headset late into the night. It's not just about winning. It's not just about gold stars and dragons. It's not just about the tokens and talismans or leveling up with supercharged mushrooms.

It's the story that captivates their attention and imagination. It's the story that gives them an "interactive narrative that they can be a part of and be whisked away by," writes Will Harris.[23] It's the setting and the scenery. It's the visuals and the graphics. It's the heroes and the villains. It's the dialogue and the subplot. It's the emotional investment and the personal involvement.

This was me, a young girl playing *Tomb Raider*, raptured into the world of Lara Croft, a character I interpreted as wielding weapons for good.[24] Lara Croft inspired the young girl in me who dreamed of being an archaeologist, of exploring other countries and cultures for the sake of cherishing their most prized possessions.

This archaeological dream of mine was inspired by a trip I took to Panama in 2007. There I was, standing shoulder to shoulder with the bare-breasted women of Ipetí Emberá—an indigenous community in eastern Panama. There, I lived with and learned from the Emberá—how to bathe in a river, how to stain ink on skin, how to tell the sacred stories of your totems, tattoos, and treasures.

I've yet to live this dream in real life. But I have lived it in a game.

The reading of fiction offers an invitation to be fascinated, to find ourselves in awe and wonder. It is an invitation to learn new stories, encounter new worlds, and envision new endings.

I once wrote a children's book for an internship, and it was a dream come true to conceptualize the idea for it—to choose the setting and the story line along with the characters.

The goal was to write a book that children could see themselves in. With animals as characters, the book did just that.

Making a simple choice like this is about so much more than simply creating characters. It's about creating a point of entry for readers to experience the story. For readers, it's about reading to both see and be seen. How powerful that we can read to see ourselves and see the world. How redemptive that we have a creative way of learning to live, lead, and love better.

"Escape [by way of reading] is the only faithful act," says Andrew Lazo. "Escape as looking at the false reality that I have been pitched, and saying *no*. There's another world, there's a new Jerusalem coming down someday. Yes, the moon will turn red and the stars will fall from the sky and the hearts of men will grow cold. But there's a better world coming."[25]

This is what fiction does for us—the reading, writing, and watching of it. This is what getting lost in a movie, or book, or play, or character, or video game does. It provides a pathway and a portal into a fantastical world that is not our own, not our home. It provides an escape from our earthly lives—all of the routines, rituals, rage, and ruin.

Fiction enchants us to believe in better endings.

Fiction compels us to fight for a better world.

On earth, as it is in heaven.

Prayer

God, inspire me to believe in the power of stories. Teach me truth through tales; help me hope because of them. Guide me with grace as I encounter conflict within my own story. Lead me to keep sight of the good ending you've already set into motion. Strengthen me as I walk this journey. Remind me that I'm never alone. Amen.

Prompts

What is one fictional work that's changed your life?

Who is one fictional character you want to be like?

Practices

Create a character. Envision their fears and their deepest longings. What tools, elements, magic systems, worlds, laws, and languages would you need to make available for your character and why? Develop this character in a poem, short story, script, video game, novel, movie, or play. Would others experience renewed hope from your story? Would they learn to believe in love, in God, in society, in self? Does your story communicate goodwill, wonder, truth, or discovery? What do you believe your character might teach our world if this character was real?

Now, create the foil of this character, a person whose characteristics and motives oppose that of your character's. What can you learn from their relationship? What is antagonistic about this character? What conflicts do they create? Are they beyond redemption? What could this character's existence teach others?

Pieces

As the controller lay firmly clasped in my grasp, I dove into a polygon-rendered landscape fit for a character formed by the creative elements of my mind. I gave him a name, and he was placed in a ring. As I smashed a combination of buttons, he wrestled his opponent the way I intended him to. Whether exuberant in victory, or exasperated in defeat, this here is a favorite childhood memory.

—Lamar Gibbs

I will tie balloons to my house

and float.

Birds, coffee, and books
will be my company
as the cleansing breeze
blows through the windows.
I will sit on the porch and
watch the sun rise and the
sun set each day.
Clouds will be my sustenance;
the rain will quench my thirst;
rainbows will be my delight.
I will land
in a forest,
in the shadow of a mountain,
and at the edge of the sea.

I will taste and see
what is there for me.
Lush green, waves, waterfalls,
wildflowers, mushrooms, lightning bugs,
grace, dolphins, dappled light, deer,
caves, quiet, apples, rocks, trees, rabbits.
My pen will record my explorations;
I will map the places my feet and
my heart take me.
When my heart is full and settled,
when my words have done all
they can to capture the treasures,
when my heart longs
to go back,
I will tie balloons to my house

and float

home.

—Bethany Howard

Let There Be Tears

Music, like all art, is the memory of virtue. No matter our setting, with imagination we can dignify it. Remake this broken world, even just a little.

—Sho Baraka, *He Saw That It Was Good*

I was born and raised a blink away from the city that never sleeps, the city where skyscrapers stretch so high you blind your eyes as the sun ricochets one hundred stories of radiant light down at your feeble frame. The city where color comes fast through cans on Brooklyn brownstones. Graffiti on walls, the urban message in a bottle, souls spilling out stories like love letters lost at sea.

New York City.

It's the skyline my soul has tried to memorize since the start of my life, since the days my dad would drive my brothers and me into Chinatown. Those were the days my mom would taxi us over the George Washington Bridge, the world's busiest bridge—tell me, where is the lie?

I am a Manhattan mural of my own—a swirl of colors, spiraling Black and White and Indigenous gold. At times, I lost myself to the many colors that made me, like the many mixed colors on a canvas that mute one another, only to make a muddied brown.

When I was young and felt lost inside the many shades of me—the art of me—music found me. Heard me. Spoke to me. I remember bare feet on cold floors, the silence of a room and a music stand spread wide with notes on pages. I practiced my violin and my flute in the quiet of the night, turning stanzas into songs, pouring out poetry from my soul.

I loved and still love all music. This comes from the influence of my dad playing albums ranging from James Taylor to Gloria Estefan. From Michael Jackson's "They Don't Care About Us" to Marvin Gaye's "Inner City Blues."

I loved all music.

All music except for jazz, that is.

Even now, vivid memories paint themselves anew across reminiscent expanses in my brain. Dad playing jazz in long car rides. Around the neighborhood, across New York's bridges. Song by song, he teaches me how to single out the sound of the saxophone. The *rat-a-tat-tat* of the drums.

"I don't like it," I'd tell him. "It gives me headaches."

And it did.

It really did hurt my head to hear the whining saxophone and the staccato of drums that never seemed to end. Jazz, as far as I was concerned, was the song that'd never end. I did not understand it—did not understand the breadth and depth of the highest highs of the flute and the lowest lows of the cello.

I didn't know then like I do now that it all means something, not only for my listening ears and my music-loving soul but it means something in the whole grand scale of humanity. There is a long legacy to lean into when it comes to jazz. Layers of lives, another swirling of colors, all woven into the same fabric that blankets over the history of Black people and White people and everyone in between.

The thing about jazz is that soul seeps out from every syncopated note. You can't listen without learning and leaning into the art and history of it all. It is a beautiful crooning and crescendo of a sound—the blaring brass, the solo cellist crying into the strings and hanging on every note. Lyrics that talk of hell on earth and that glorious home in the sky.

These songs hinge onto our history, as if to say I am holding on to horror and yet still holding on to hope.

The juxtaposition of jazz is that it is a lovely sound but also a longing sound. In jazz the tension heard is also a tension lived and felt. Those songs you hear, so soulfully beautiful, are also filled with a deep, dark sorrow.

One group of people that understood the slow, secret seeping of sorrow was African Americans who waited *and* waded through the bondage of burdens and beatings that came because of the color of their skin. This is where jazz comes in.

This is where the blues begins.

Naomi Ruth Floyd, vocalist and composer, spoke this truth in her seminar at the Hutchmoot Conference in 2020. I listened in on her session from the barn at my friend Meredith's house. The two of us, masked and sitting six feet apart, were equally stunned and in awe of the words flowing from Floyd's lips.

"The blues were birthed as a way of expressing through music that sense of the profound loss, grief, abandonment, loneliness, and suffering that comes with being a perpetual sojourner in a strange land."[1]

The blues.

Music that expresses loss, grief, abandonment, loneliness, and suffering.

Songs that croon words about the back-breaking work of living in a land but never being a part of it. Living in a land and yet still straining to see the love in it. Living in a land and yet longing for a way out of it.

There is only so much torment and turmoil a human soul can take, only so much toil that a human body can weather before it breaks, bends under the will and might of another, begins to lose belief in the possibility of a better world or a loving God.

There is only so much torment and turmoil a human soul can take before it begins to bleed the broken out. Sometimes, the only way to bleed the broken out is through language, language that comes out in riffs and rhythm because, sometimes, the release of it also needs to bring relief with it.

Music will always be a release.

Music will always bring relief.

At the 1964 Berlin Jazz Festival, Martin Luther King Jr. said:

God has wrought many things out of oppression. He has endowed his creatures with the capacity to create and from this capacity has flowed the sweet songs of sorrow and joy that have allowed man to cope with his environment and many different situations.[2]

In his speech, Martin Luther King Jr. goes on to say that before writers and scholars had begun to process the presence of racial tensions, "musicians were returning to their roots to affirm that which was stirring within their souls."[3]

It was music—always has been, always will be. While the words may vary, the theme remains the same: hope rising up and out of hardship. The proclamation of light and life in the midst of darkness, in the midst of death. I know this myself, a girl of so many shades, conflicted about where to begin and who to be. I found myself mending through music in a way no other art form has offered. I found myself soothed through sorrow seeped out in song.

This is why the Psalms both break and mend our hearts. The collection is not only holy but it is wholly human. Line after line of horror and heartbreak, the people of God—sojourners seeking for some sure sign of God—profess their heartbreak and pour out their lament to ask *how long*.

How long will the suffering endure? When will the world tilt and turn under a new kind of sun—the kind that doesn't scorch, that doesn't beat, that doesn't bring beads of sweat to drip from the brow? *How long* is also the question the psalmist asks in Psalm 13:1–6.

> How long, LORD? Will you forget me forever?
> How long will you hide your face from me?
> How long must I wrestle with my thoughts
> and day after day have sorrow in my heart?
> How long will my enemy triumph over me?
> Look on me and answer, LORD my God.
> Give light to my eyes, or I will sleep in death,
> and my enemy will say, "I have overcome him,"
> and my foes will rejoice when I fall.

But I trust in your unfailing love;
    my heart rejoices in your salvation.
I will sing the LORD's praise,
    for he has been good to me.

The Psalms, the blues, and jazz alike are the rhythmic releasing of emotional ruin. They are the sound of God's people reaching for relief, and we, too, are called to take part in this kind of cathartic creativity.

It is good to name our places of pain, our histories of horror. It is good to give rise to them—to admit the depths of darkness, the depressions that hollow holes into our hearts. There is space and there is faith enough to lift loud these depths—every individual and collective trauma and tragedy.

And the truth about mending through music is that it cannot be contained to jazz. The ability for a heart and soul to find freedom through song extends beyond genre and reaches deep into the core of the craft. It is an ordering of that which is chaotic; it is organized breath pushing back the boundary of darkness.

"When life itself offers no order and meaning, the musician creates order and meaning from the sounds of the earth which flow through his instrument," remarks Dr. Martin Luther King Jr.[4]

This is why and how the ministry of music goes beyond the bellowing of the blues. This is why it can also be seen through the work of Dmitri Shostakovich, a Soviet-era Russian who composed *Symphony No. 13*. This symphony's first movement, "Babi Yar," is a bone-chilling melody that served as a song to show solidarity with the Jewish people who suffered under the oppression of Stalin.[5]

Beyond "Babi Yar," Shostakovich is known for orchestrating compositions that resonate with complexity and conflict, as felt through the sustaining of deep, dark notes.

Nicholas Cannariato writes about Stephen Johnson, a music broadcaster who authored the book *How Shostakovich Changed My Mind*, which explores Shostakovich's music. Elaborating on Johnson's words, Cannariato writes that Shostakovich's music ultimately gave form to the feelings of those who suffered, and that, "in giving form to feelings, music can move someone from emotional confinement to an abiding sense of belonging—in war and in peace."[6]

There are so many other songs and scenarios filled with suffering, I could write a separate book on them. America is not the only country that aches. Suffering is not only personal—it's universal.

There is Germany and the history of the Holocaust. Oh, how I remember standing with my own two feet, some ten years ago, at the Neuengamme concentration camp with my friend Lara and her mom, Astrid.

They'd spent days and weeks showing me around Germany, from the Ahrensburg Palace to Lübeck and every bakery in between. Then, they brought me to Neuengamme—a place that holds the hurt history of their beloved country.

There I was, standing on land that held the weight of innocent lives lost. In the hallowed silence, I could feel the scream of a thousand voices crying out. I imagined the despair; I imagined the death; I imagined the sorrow.

I eventually came to learn that music occupied that same space that once echoed with the sounds of suffering.

There was also a fair amount of spontaneous, clandestine music-making in the barracks of Neuengamme. . . . Many prisoners composed songs for themselves and their bunk-mates. Other individual musicians would give casual concerts in the evenings or on weekends. Heinz Dörmer, a musically gifted amateur who had been in the camp since October 1940, was frequently asked to perform in various blocks throughout the camp. He recited or sang ballads, poems or couplets, sometimes accompanied by members of the [prisoner] orchestra.[7]

In the midst of pain, the prisoners at Neuengamme created and gave "form to feeling," as Cannariato says.[8]

Might it be that in art and in song we too can give form to our feelings? Might we help *others* move from their painful prisons to the truth of their belovedness—to belonging, to breathing easier—even *while* wars wage on.

You can sing your way through sorrow and be surprised to find yourself sustained *in* sorrow. This is the paradox of the faith we profess.

Though there are people and places and purposes set on bending your bones, they do not have to break your spirit. Through song, you can carry on through the deepest well of suffering. Through singing, you can beckon others to carry on through the wells of their deepest mourning. Those songs you're uploading to TikTok and YouTube, and those recordings you think are just floating around in a virtual universe of videos—they might touch the life of someone you'll never know. They might lift *your* life even as sorrow lingers.

This is the very foundation of the Christian faith. Believers set their sights on things above (see Col. 3:2) and strain their eyes to see beyond momentary suffering (see 2 Cor. 4:17).

Christ, too, knew what it meant to suffer. Christ, too, knew what it meant to carry on through sorrow, all the while stretching out hands for a new tomorrow.

"The greatest grief, shown in the Bible, delivers the greatest blues line uttered from the world's greatest blues singer," says Naomi Ruth Floyd. "Not the remarkable Ma Rainey, not the great Bessie Smith, but from Jesus himself on the cross. Jesus, the ultimate blues singer, sings the greatest blues line ever uttered: 'My God, my God, why hast thou forsaken me?' These words reflect deep abandonment, loss, and utter despair. Jesus cries out in agony about his struggle of separation from his father even *while* enduring it."[9]

Jesus knew what it felt like to be crushed under the weight of oppression, hurt by the hands of those he loved, betrayed by his brother, rejected by the ones he reached out his hands to, and broken even while believing in and for something better.

This is why it matters, undoubtedly matters, for you to create and make and sing the songs that you do. Your art is an act of defiance; it is your faith on display. It brings hope for today and hope for tomorrow.

Through oppression, depression, every expression and question, it matters to write and paint and dance; it matters to sing and give sound to that which weighs on your soul.

The world may tell you that you are damned to your depression, that your days will be filled with waking and walking with your sorrow, but not through it. You might step into family gatherings, friendship circles, meetings with therapists, and prayer nights in the pews of churches, and you will begin to tell your story of suffering—or that of your people—only to be told that your story is not true. That it is either a lie or a liability and that there is therefore no room for your truth.

You and your story of suffering, whether it be about your body or within your body, may be shunned and shut down and suppressed. You may be told to submit to a different kind of story, to just another kind of slavery of the soul.

It is then and there, in these moments and places and churches and homes and classrooms and seasons, that you must unearth and unleash the kind of courageous creativity that will not only seep out your story but save your soul.

And you will cry and confess the certain kind of hardship you have endured. And your tears will water the ground that has been broken. And the seed of your strength will someday emerge. It will grow and flower with hope, the kind of longing that looks toward the future.

You will bend and you will break but you will not bow to the push of darkness, to the swell of hopelessness.

Let there be tears, *yes*, but let there also be tenacity. Let there be truth sang by tenors, lyrics with love, and choruses of courage.

Let there be an awakening of the dawn, the grand opening of the sky, so bright with the light of life, so luminescent, that it paints over the gloom, paints a new story, a new ending.

If not for the here and now, then, *hallelujah*, for some day.

Prayer

God, look at me with love, for I cannot whisper halle-lujah. Speak to me softly, for I am weary from hearing the sounds of war, both within me and in my world. In my depression, in my despair, in my tensions, and in my traumas, remind me that you are here. Tune my heart to climb from hurt to hope, from the sorrow of the night to the joy of the morning. Revive my spirit, God, and do not turn your face away. Amen.

Prompts

What are the horrors you need to release?

What is the hope you need to reclaim?

Practices

Light a candle and create a Spotify playlist. Curate a list of soothing songs, a soundtrack to sing your way through sorrow *and* toward hope.

Share your playlist with your people. Let them join the choir of your lamenting as well as the chorus of your hopeful hallelujahs.

Pieces

A tear rolls slowly
Off the tips of
My eyelashes
Mingling
The pain and the joy
With pure exhaustion.
Failure and triumph
Beauty and anguish
Roiling together
Inside my chest and
Releasing itself
Compressed into one
Hot, tiny tear.
Oh the emotion
Captured
In that one tiny drop
Of myself poured out.
And He holds every one
Of my tears
In a bottle.

—Alesha Sinks

Sometimes words are scalpels,
sometimes balm—
sharp, soft, ever-breathing
currents into
dead spaces.

Sometimes they are fog
clouding my sight until

I parse them out
on paper.

Sometimes the more
words I use the
less they mean.

Sometimes tears flow
faster than words.

Sometimes, I get tired.

Sometimes,

you too?

Or maybe,

just me.

—Rachel Steffan

9

Let There Be Breath

Listen, are you breathing just a little, and calling it a life?

—Mary Oliver, *Devotions:*
The Selected Poems of Mary Oliver

In my mind, I die every day.

Sometimes I see scenes of me bleeding out, usually from the brain, but sometimes from the stomach too. It is always a vision of me just standing there, and then I'm falling out, blood leaking, heart slowing, eyes closing, life fading.

Bed sheets.

This is the place where I wake up, where I wage the visions in my mind. I stumble out of bed, and I proceed to wait for the snapshots to move across my mind. Glimpses of the irrational, all the ways in which I will die, stamped out for me—at least six impossible ways all before breakfast.

I've died from bites by venomous snakes and poisonous spiders, from my heart falling into my stomach, my head collapsing onto my neck, my stomach exploding toxins into my blood-stream, car accidents, bombs in the city, homicide, assault. I've died every possible way, and I've been alive to watch each one.

You can call it hypochondria; I call it being human.

These images didn't come flooding into my mind until after a season of sickness, a sickness that I still don't have answers for. I know it was the first initial flush that had triggered my brain to be alarmed at any slight trickling of change in my body. The many months after my first "episode," as my husband, Shin, and I call them, were just as much a mental battle as they were a physical one.

I am still working on letting the light of God's truth chase out the dark of this lie. I am still working on allowing his truth, and the very reality that I *am* alive, to transform and renew my mind. I am still working on releasing the fear of some impending, irrational death. I am still working on living in peace and enjoying my days so that if and when I die—be it irrational or not—my soul will be at perfect peace.

Maybe this is you too. Maybe you're learning to live with the light on. Maybe you're learning to open the windows and air out the spaces in which you swell and dream and sometimes fear. Maybe you are learning to let go of the stale thoughts within your mind; maybe you are gasping to breathe in new, fresh air.

Peace.

***

The first time I had an anxiety attack, I found myself heaving and gasping for air. In no less than five minutes after walking out of a senior seminar—in which we had been invited to celebrate our upcoming graduation—I was told to look forward to paying back the grand sum of my student debts, all fifty thousand dollars deep.

I stopped outside, my head spinning with numbers and the promise of debt collectors chasing me down after six months. I swung open the door of my then-boyfriend's car. He watched as I heaved, mentioned something about the Bible and praying, all the while watching the rise and fall of my chest as I could not speak, could not reason, could not breathe.

It was the numbers, I now know, and not knowing what to do with them. This is what eventually spiraled me into a season of anxiety—of weight loss, of deficiencies so deep it developed into dark bags beneath my eyes. This is when I found myself at the doctor's office, the nervous wreck that I was, fumbling on the table with the tissue paper crinkling, that wretched, deafening sound.

In the doctor's office, I sat there, feet dangling and goosebumps breaking out on my skin. Thoughts streamed inside my mind, inflicting jabs to every other imperfection bound to be found by her, the doctor, knocking on the door and stepping into the room, giving me her name and reaching out her hand to save me, *like I needed saving.*

She probed, and I spoke. I fumbled back and forth between twiddling my fingers and clasping the gown across my chest. I shared with her my concerns about my fatigue and the emotional pigsty I'd been. I told her about how chaotic my body had been, how things felt out of control and how *I* felt out of control.

I could barely keep from crying, let alone keep my breath to a silent whimper, before the tears were rolling and the tissue paper was crinkling and I was weeping and falling apart and unraveling in that ugly, undignified gown.

She drew a tissue, then two, then three. She handed them to me, all the while gazing into my eyes, as if it was my soul she saw drowning inside them, as if something inside needed saving.

"Breathe," she said. "You're overwhelmed and you have a lot on your plate. Take a moment each day, and just breathe. *Just breathe.*" Then she handed me a slip with information on the nearest Center for Stress Reduction, *thank you very much.*

And I wonder about you, whether you know the same. I wonder if you know that you can learn to breathe, *really* breathe. I wonder if you know that you can be, *really* be. I wonder if there is anyone there with you, handing you tissues and hugging you until the weight you bear unfolds.

I wonder if you know that you can cry, that, whether a doctor has diagnosed you or not, you can confess the actuality of your anxieties—the worries that keep you wide awake at night, the kind that run rampant in your mind, hold you hostage in the home of your body.

I am sure that you have tried so hard to keep the waves from whiplashing, to keep the wild waters from spilling out and into the other spaces in your life. But, you and I, we both know that you cannot keep on this way.

This is your actual breath that is labored, not a set of hypothetical heaving lungs. You might have forgotten your breath, forgotten that you are human and how to breathe. But you can learn again to inhale and exhale. You can live and be in rhythm with the rise and release of air in and through your lungs.

Though darkness be present, your breath can be persistent. Though wild waves and waters rage, your lungs do not have to be encaged. It is work, but it is always worth it. To believe that you can be as God is—creating the light and pushing back darkness.

Light for you,
light from you.
Breath by breath,
by heaving breath.

Some years ago, I learned a lesson on breathing in the choir room where my teacher, Ms. Phelps, would stand and dance her hands across keys of black and white.

Every comma is a call to pause for breath, she'd say, as we sang our way through Handel's *Messiah* and Mozart's *Requiem in D Minor, K. 626.* Once I noticed the commas, I could not unsee them, could not unsee how the sheet music was splattered with them.

I'd realized the same as a flutist—that breath went before every blow of a note. I knew that breath was not a thing I could keep on the back burner of my brain. To sustain a song, to blow into my Bundy flute and make music, I had to inhale. I had to exhale. I had to breathe.

I'd learned that every comma—different from a full rest, which can last as many measures as a composer determines—is a brief pause from the previous phrase and a moment to prepare before going into the next. It is a stolen moment that the audience never sees and rarely senses. It is not a part of the performance; it is for the player.

It is for *you.*

Isn't it sort of poetic and spiritual, the implication of a comma and what it means for us? That we need more than just long moments of extended rest and deep breaths? What really sustains and keeps us going are the momentary reminders to keep a steady, rhythmic pace of rest. What we want, and what we know we need, is a constant filling up of the lungs.

The American Lung Association says that "we breathe an estimated 17,000 breaths a day," most of which are inhales amounting to enough air to fill a swimming pool.[1] This fact gives us enough to know that we should ground ourselves in a practice that, literally, sustains our lives.

We already know that resting our bodies through rhythmic breath—the kind that reaches deep—helps regulate our brains to stay calm, to relieve stress. But how can we do this in ways other than what we've already been taught and told? How else can we do this beyond praying or reciting Scripture? Not to say that prayer and Scripture aren't helpful. But it is to say they aren't the only way.

We can go beyond praying prayers.

We can go beyond speaking Scriptures.

We can embrace the gift of creative expression.

We can experience the alleviation of our anxiety through art.

Think of the exhale of an instrument, the clarinet or trumpet you played in your youth. Think of the concerts and rehearsals and how you operated on breath alone. Think about how the very thing you were doing was teaching your body to regulate breath. All the while, as you were *playing*, you were training your breath. You were teaching your brain to send the message to your muscles to contract and relax. You were teaching your lungs to inhale and your learning lips to exhale.

You are an adult now, and there might not be any recitals or concerts. There might not be one-on-one lessons to show the teacher the scales you've learned or your moving hands across the valves of that trumpet.

You may no longer have the brass, but, by God, you have the breath.

And you can punctuate your days with commas—on the front porch, on lunch between shifts for work, in those first moments after you wake, while you drink down coffee, or at night when the kids are finally in bed. There can be relief, even when there is no remedy for the things that threaten your peace.

Like a musician making muscles move the flow of air in and through the hallowed space of his body—you, too, can breathe. You can conduct breath like a conductor; *you* can control the cacophony of chaos both within and around you.

The symphony of your life will rise with harsh notes and fall with harmonies too hard to hear. There will be days when washing down white pills can't stop the whirling world within. There will be days when the holy pages of the Bible cannot come fast enough, deep enough, sure enough.

But there is this—an invitation to, at the very least, catch your breath and calm your body. There is an invitation to pick up something to play, some way to purposefully position yourself to punctuate your days with the rhythm of rest.

There is a dare to return to the instrument of your past or to pick up a new one. To muster up a renewed courage to take a class in that music shop on the main street of your small town.

It might be time to reconsider all the ways you try to calm your chaotic breathing—the hyperventilating that you never can quite get under control.

It might be time to return to the music that soothes you, to once again listen to CDs from start to finish, to play soundtracks of movies, to whisper the names of symphonies under your breath.

This is your pass to press pause, your permission slip to lose yourself to an endless loop of YouTube videos as you search for the songs that soothe your soul—Andrea Bocelli and Sarah Brightman singing "Time to Say Goodnight," or Celine Dion singing "The Prayer," or Whitney Houston, Mariah Carey, Carrie Underwood, Donnie McClurkin.

This is your call to go and listen for the seeping of breath by Joy Harjo or Immanuel Wilkins on the saxophone or Bobbi Humphrey on the flute. This is your reminder to watch the bagpipe players the next time you are at a renaissance festival—watch the way in which they breathe, how they draw air in deep.

It is all a conduction—an orchestrated control, a calm of breath. Every inhale and exhale is a sure sign that you are still here, still holding on to life.

Even when you do not feel whole, even when the house of your body still trembles exhausted, even when your world spins and your lungs heave, you can calm raging seas by just learning to breathe.

May you find inhale through these words by Christina Williams, of Fallow Ink:

> Learn to breathe; draw
> Your now-ness
> Into the nestling of your ribs.
>
> Breathe
>
> Breathe.
>
> Take as much time as you need.
>
> Then shape the soul words
> Until they sing
> Softer
> In your mouth
> I am here
> I am here   I am here
> I am here

Prayer

Dear God, you know every trembling breath on my lips. Help me to feel the tension in my body, help me to sense when stress overwhelms. Calm me to courage; slow my breath, steady my body, soothe my soul. Remind me to believe that peace is for me, and teach me to pursue the practice of it. Amen.

Prompts

What brings your breath to chaos?

What brings your breath to calm?

Practices

Light a candle and prepare your ears and heart to hear. Listen to the song "A Model of the Universe" by the late Jóhann Jóhannsson from the original soundtrack for *The Theory of Everything.* Listen to the ebb and flow of the piano, the swell of the strings. Listen for the fall of the song—the moment that sounds like the song is ending. Here begins an acoustic rendering of the same melody. Bend your ears to hear the player breathing. You will hear deep inhales, full exhales. Though he is not breathing into a woodwind instrument or taking breaths during moments of rest, your sensitivity to hearing him breathe can be a pathway to understanding the power of calm, controlled breath.

Play the song again and breathe while you listen.

Pieces

There's rhythm in letting go
    In trusting the greater picture
And moving in your own flow
The people in our lives
Who bring a certain kind of harmony
Just by their unique wiring
    There's a rhythm behind the changing seasons
    And the space between
That's knitting together a deeper unity
Despite any rhyme or reason
The frequency of a heart beat
The rise and fall of a chest
Exhaling fear, inhaling faith
Breathing in the fullness of this human experience

—Joy Antonio

Spirit filled air, it's light and invincible.
Yet bears love and grace.
What was created to bring me life
was abandoned.
Cemented in my body,
blocked in and awaiting to burst.
Why do I hold onto something
that was designed to freely flow?
Anxiety, stress, and bitterness binds it
to my broken body.
To take breath is an art that has been forgotten.

Take me back to when all I needed was a breath to exist.

—Dora Moua

10

Let There Be Movement

As a dancer, my body is my instrument. I speak to the audience through every muscle and tendon, with every glissade and renversé.

—Misty Copeland, *Ballerina Body*

I am in my car, parked by the border of a body of water, and I have spent the better part of the morning wrestling with my writing. I have been thinking and overthinking of all the ways that I can move my words, of how I can place them together to make this book blaze and burn with truth.

Instead, it is my hand that burns and my arm that aches. There is a dull pain that will not go away, and this is how it has been for the last year any time I've picked up the pen to write or held a camera in the hollow of my hand.

I look out to the water, the man-made lake that I've heard has a whole city buried beneath. I look out toward the boats, the

126

pontoons, and the cruisers scattered along a dock of wooden boards all perfectly placed together.

Lake Norman.

A body of water, birthed from the slow trickle of the Catawba River, swelling up to create the lake that so many have come to love. And though I love it too, it also aches to stare out into the expanse of this land turned lake.

Looking out at the lake is like looking out at myself, like seeing the slow swell beneath the surface of my own skin. My swollen hands, my swollen feet. The landscape that drowns under the body of water I've become.

I do not know what came first, the 26 mm nodule lodged into my neck or the broken thyroid that fails to push a rage of hormones in and through my body. My body is not what it used to be. My voice is frail and weak, and I often speak with strain.

Sometimes, I reach out my hand to hold a pencil only for it to cripple up with pain, to debilitate the penning of my poems, prose, and pieces.

But this is not the first time my body swelled with sickness, not the first time I felt a strain in my voice that left me mouthing the words in chorus more than I sang them. There was the time in high school when I learned I had rheumatic fever— a rheumatism caused by untreated strep throat that releases trigger-happy antibodies that betray and attack your own body.

When my doctor found the inflammation in my hips, it all made sense. It made sense why my knees gave out when I put pressure on them every time I pitched in softball. It made sense why I sat out on the sidelines at basketball games when I could not cheer because I had no voice. It made sense, the surge of heat that swelled in my body and the way I could pinpoint the hurt in my hands, the pain in my elbow, the hurt in my hips.

Those were the days I hid away in the piano rooms, tucked between the choir and symphonic band room. Those were the days I'd taught myself to play notes and chords and songs on the piano, like "Down by the Sally Gardens" and "Danny Boy."

Those were the days I learned to write my own songs, songs that seemed to soothe my voice instead of straining it.

I moved my hands to make music in an attempt to heal the hurt I held within. And, while the making of music mended my soul, the truth is that the making hurt. My bones, muscles, and every ligament in between had hurt.

We use our bodies for everything—to build houses, to birth babies, to bake bread, to burn wood. We use our strength; we use our breath; we use our muscles; we use every cell and every vein.

But sometimes bodies break. Sometimes our feet cannot carry the weight of all we are. Sometimes lungs cannot hold air. Sometimes hands cannot hug porcelain mugs or other human hands. Sometimes, even the hollow of a pen is too much for a hurting hand to hold.

This is when the act of making is hard, when the art of creating, in turn, aches beyond the skin over our bones.

I cannot help but wonder if you know these aches, if the act of your making has been hard too. I wonder, even now, if you are on your bed with a baby or a child or a parent or a grandparent whose body is too small or too weak or too heavy to sustain strength. I wonder if you are the one taking care of them and if their pain has mingled with the ache of your own soul.

I wonder if the burden of their body has made the making hard for you. I wonder if you've come to believe that you cannot cradle the broken body of another while you create. I wonder if you've given into believing that the two cannot coincide, that there could never be time or truth or trust enough to reach out your hands and hold the tension of these two things together.

I wonder if it's your own body that has betrayed you and if it has been this way since birth or if the brokenness came bursting through without rhyme or reason. I wonder if you might be able to behold the reflection of your face, stare lovingly into your eyes and tell the truth—tell yourself that you are not too broken to make beautiful things. Your body may be different than it was before, but there is still time, and there are still tools, and there is still space and grace enough to discover new ways of awakening your soul to stretch and reach for art.

It may very well be that your illness is invisible, that your disability doesn't draw attention—that it hides the fact that your health is not as it should or could be. There might be a particular part of you that is prone to pain and that not one person could pinpoint the truth of this by beholding you from the outside, simply by seeing you for your skin and not the resilient soul that you are.

It may be your swollen brain, it may be your bad blood, it may be your scaly skin, it may be your thinning hair, it may be your sugar levels, it may be your frail bones, it may be the growing tumors—both benign and malignant—it may be your hands, your legs, the small drum in your ear, your seizing body, or the blur in your eyes.

Whatever the sickness, wherever the pain, however seemingly insignificant you deem it is or is not, if something in you has made the making hard—if something in you has exasperated the experience, has caused confusion to cloud over this call to create—then here is a truth to behold, a new story to be told.

There can be healing in the midst of this hurt and hollowness, a healing that looks like wholeness, even when it does not look like a whole new body. There *is* a way and, though it be different, it *is* there, all right there for you.

Can you become again? Can you turn your face to a new truth? Can you do something different or differently and find that you love it all the same, find that there is still pleasure and purpose to be held and to be had?

Even now, right this breathing moment, I am not typing these words onto my computer. I am *speaking* them into a phone. I am speaking and spilling them onto the page. This is what I do when my brain can't keep up; this is what I do when my hands hurt.

This reminds me of theoretical physicist and cosmologist Stephen Hawking, whose bones and body betrayed him too. Yet he still found a way to release the words within him. Through computers connected to speech synthesizers, and then later a "cheek switch" that "could detect, via a low infrared beam, when Hawking tensed his cheek muscle," Hawking—by moving one, mere muscle—wrote out and authored his theories and thoughts.[1]

There was disease in his cells, but he *discovered* through it.

There was slurring in his speech, but he *spoke* through it.

There was paralysis in his muscles, but he *pushed* through it.

There was chaos in his body, but he *created* through it.

There is a video that surfaced, or resurfaced, on social media in the middle of the COVID-19 pandemic. It's a video of an elderly woman living with memory loss. In the video, symphonic music swells with the sound of *Swan Lake* by Pyotr Ilyich Tchaikovsky and, gradually, the woman gracefully moves her hands.

Then, a crescendo—suddenly, she spreads her hands outward and to her side. She bows like a swan, unbound by disease, and becomes an elegant ballerina once again. For that brief moment, her memory recalls the movements that her muscles once knew.[2]

I cannot tell you about what I cannot see, about the neuroscience of surging synapses in this woman's brain and how they might have awakened her memory to dance. I cannot tell you what I do not know about psychology and pathways of pain. I cannot profess to you that I am a professional. I am no doctor, no scientist, no expert in any areas of embodiment.

But I can tell you what I have seen—how a beautiful woman, bound in her body and bound in her brain, made movement through her muscles, anyway.

While I do not know the make of your muscles, the diagnosis of your disease(s), the state of your sickness, what I do know is that creativity is not bound to what you create, it extends to *how* you create. It extends to the way in which you navigate the actual process of creating. It is cultivated when you resolve to move forward in *how* you adapt in the expression of your experiences, your emotions, your embodiment, and all else that pertains to the person you are.

It might be time to move your body, time to move your focus on what you *can* do. It might be time to be surprised by all the ways that you *can* express yourself—all the endless ways that you *can* release art, portray your passion, move your muscles, and dance around new discoveries.

You may come to find in this journey that your making might not look like the art you were once used to.

You might move lightly, speak slowly, play softly, write briefly, think only. You may not ever pick up the pen or paintbrush

131

again. You may find yourself moving on to simpler skills, or a different kind of craft that caters to you in this season.

Jennifer Ji-Hye Ko, a writer and poet of Fallow Ink, typically finds relief in the release of words, reprieve in writing out sound and sense. While her physical body often feels bound and broken, she also has her days when it is hard to even think of stringing together sentences. There was a time, through Fallow Ink, when she turned to simple *movement* in order to unleash the art her soul was longing to release. Of this moment, she writes:

> Words are hard to come by these days so, inspired by my wedding photo en pointe on a swing, I'm tapping into my past life as a dancer and filtering it through my current limitations. I introduce to you my dancing feet (while the rest of me sinks into the bed) to one of my favorite hymns, "Just As I Am" written by disabled hymnist, Charlotte Elliott, and performed by Johnny Cash.

Along with this piece on Instagram, Jennifer posted a video that captured just her legs, swung down by her bedside. In the video, she is stretching her toes, moving them slowly, one by one.

No *plié*.

No *arabesque*.

Just her legs swung low to the floor. Just her, bedridden and broken but bravely bringing herself to move, to express, to embody, to release, to *create*.

Jennifer's words are not the only words on Instagram that have helped me behold the beauty of broken bodies, the beauty of my own broken body.

One day, scrolling through my Instagram feed, I see a stunning picture of my friend K.J. Ramsey. She is wearing a bright, blue shirt and a mini scarf around her neck. She is smiling and there are mountains in the distance. And there is water at her feet. The blue sky undulates behind her.

In her post, she shares about Ankylosing Spondylitis—the disease that causes pain to swell and swirl inside her spine, inside her body. She writes of Eugene Peterson who, in his book *The Practice of Resurrection*, says that it is a worthy habit to look into the mirror and call ourselves *Saint*. In a candid reflection, my beautiful, brave friend writes:

> I started blessing
> what I had been avoiding.
>
> Saint, in my skin.
> Saint, in my sin.
> Saint, in my struggle.
>
> I started seeing
> the swelling of my skin
> as the story of my resilience.
>
> I started holding
> the pills in my hand
> as prayers of perseverance.
>
> I started naming
> my imperfect reflection in the mirror
> as ineffaceable in glory and goodness.
>
> This tender flesh is chosen and always loved,
> a walking miracle of grace and grit.
>
> All its swelling and shrinking is but stretching
> to hold the mystery of being embraced by Jesus
> and renamed as beloved by the Father with Christ.

Stop turning away from that which God is always
turned toward.

See your skin and say your name:
Saint. Saint. Saint.

I can barely speak, let alone read, K.J.'s stunning words without a chill setting in over the swell of my skin. The words move me, even as I move through the messy middle of my own medical journey. Even as I find myself in the care of doctors poking my veins and drawing my blood. Even as I wake to the ache that stretches from my arm to my chest, to my wanting hands that wish to write and pour out words—hands that wish to make without end, without limitation, without restraint.

I wake and stare into the mirror, only to see a reflection of symptoms that make no sense, a story of suffering that "lingers," as K.J. would call it.

I see the tired under my eyes, the tired *in* my eyes, the tension on my lips, the roundness of my puffy face. I see through my swollen skin and the headaches that no one else sees, the pills that I push down, the prayers in which I plead.

Saint, in my skin, I say.

Saint, in my skin, I will always need to say.

It's the benediction you need, too, as you fold from this chapter and into the next. It is the benediction you need because the suffering you are standing in may very well continue beyond the paragraphs on this page.

I know this is true for you because it is true for me too. We will walk away from these words, and we will still rise in pain, and our bodies will still rage broken and wrinkled and aged.

We will still stretch out our hands to swallow sticky, white pills that drag down the esophagus, drop down to the pits of our ulcered stomachs.

I hope you recite these words as you sit in silent rooms and wait for doctors in white coats. I hope you recite these words in empty cars, in bathroom stalls, on sunken couches, before brimming sinks and foggy mirrors.

I hope that, even if you cannot create the art you wish, you might come to believe that your body is making. I hope that, in times when you are aware of it and in times when you are not, you'd come to believe that your body is making—making blood, making oxygen, making nutrients, making breath.

Yes.

Even when your hands cannot create, your body already is. Even when your body cannot dance, your blood already is. You, *yourself*, are already a work of art. Stand in awe of you, the art that has been made and is in the making.

It is a radical act of will, to believe that you are a work of art.

And believing in this truth is a radical act of worship.

Prayer

God, my body hurts and my spirit is weak. When it is hard to hear and feel and sense you, remind me that you are near. When it is hard to walk and see and find you, remind me you are here. Hold me in my physical pain, hold me as my tired body ages. Remind me who you are. Help me whisper out the word that claims my wholeness and worth: Saint. Amen.

Prompts

How have you cursed your body?
How can you bless your body?

Practices

Move your muscles, even the smallest one possible. Move your whole body if it's a good day. Move, even if it's just the parts that can muster up strength today. Dance if you can. Record your reflections. Was the moving hard? Was it helpful? Was it freeing? If you cannot write with a pen (due to pain or physical limitations), write using a dictation app. Reread or listen to your reflections. Bless your body for the bravery of its movement.

Spine poetry—for when your body is broken, the back cannot move, and the blood count is thin. Use what you have—books. Take the strong spines of books and curate the titles together to construct a poem. Borrow the strength of books and their words when you do not or cannot create your own.

Pieces

I intended to paint a sunset.

I made some mistakes. I had some fun. I ended up with something beautiful anyway.

Maybe that's life. I certainly never imagined I'd have a life so constrained by chronic pain. This wasn't the dream. These were not the raw materials I expected to be working with. This life hasn't gone the way I expected. But, there is freedom to be found in abandoning the plan and going with the flow. There is joy. Even this can be—and is—a beautiful life.

—Tiffany Najbart

My bed has been a cocoon, wrapping me, warm, and aching; bones cracking and strumming tendons as I squirm. My bed has been a chrysalis, wrapping me, snug and suffocating: my soul leathered and softened by slow metamorphosis. When I finally emerge, I'll be completely new.

—Jennifer Ji-Hye Ko

11

Let There Be Silence

Sabbath is not just rest from making things. It's rest from the need to make something of ourselves.

—Rich Villodas, *The Deeply Formed Life*

There isn't a day that goes by when I don't hear the same song in my head, the same sound of ringing in my ears, a static clang and clamor of bells in dissonant disarray.

For years I'd heard the ringing, but it would come and it would go. Now, for whatever rhyme or reason, my ears ring without end, with no sure sign of stopping.

At my desk.

On March 20, 2021, I am at my computer, in the middle of the night, writing these words to send them off in a newsletter.

I wake in the middle of the night to feed my newborn. Every night is the same—the world is dark and quiet and fast asleep, but my head is loud and busy and wide awake. Except, this past night was different. In the quiet of the night, I was finally quiet in the soul. I might not know what thoughts or sounds come rushing and rising to the surface in the moments *you* try to find or make pause, but this I do know. I know that the only way to really rise up and out of the ashes is to allow yourself to pursue moments of pause. I can't tell you when and why to pause, I can only tell you *how*. I can tell you that your pausing doesn't have to be perfect for it to be powerful. *I have tinnitus.* Which is just a dressed-up word for saying that my ears resound with the ringing echo of chimes and bells, all day, every day. So, my pausing is never perfect. It is never calm or quiet or ideal; it is always loud and swarming and exhausting. But I believe in a God who is intricately involved and compassionately concerned with the health of my head space. And I believe that the more we pause, the more we welcome God. The more we yield, the more we say *yes* to his hand in our hearts.

There is a kind of creativity that is cultivated not by production but by pausing. A kind of practice that brings forth creation by way of absence *more* than mere presence. The best way to explain this is to liken it to the cycles that can be seen in a garden—the seasons that swell with abundance on the surface because of the seeds buried beneath the surface of the dark, deeply hidden earth. Seeds under the surface of the soil, sunken into a certain kind of silence.

Silence.

It is a word that our culture has grown uncomfortable with. The truth about silence and why we don't like it is that, oftentimes, the silence we find ourselves in is not silent at all. Usually it ends up being stimulated and anything but still. In fact, there are times when it feels as though the silence is deafeningly loud, like it is more distracting than the noise we drown ourselves in. Sometimes, silence is more of a scream and a yell than a peaceful well of quiet.

A few months after the come-and-go of my tinnitus had settled into permanence, I watched the movie *The Sound of Metal*. It's about a fictional character named Ruben Stone, as played by Riz Ahmed. Ruben is a drummer in a heavy metal rock band who suddenly loses his hearing. He learns from his doctor that he should leave his band, undergo more testing, and avoid exposure to loud sounds. Concerned about his hearing, and ultimately relapsing during his sobriety, Ruben makes the reluctant decision to join a rural shelter for deaf recovering addicts. Here, though his goal is to learn to live with silence, he continues to cling to the hope of one day hearing again.

In time, Ruben tries his hand at a desperate attempt to restore his hearing. He spends everything he has to undergo surgery for a cochlear implant, which ultimately fails and leaves him hearing the tortured sound of distortion and static—the sound of *metal*.

The movie ends with Ruben walking alone and making his way toward a bench surrounded by the clamorous sound of conversation, cars whizzing, and church bells ringing with radio-like static. The scene is loud and obnoxious; it is painful to hear. Every sound, as heard by Ruben, is amplified by the resonance of its own echo.

Then the scene cuts to Ruben sitting still on the bench and removing his hearing aid. Flowers are rustling, people are walking and talking, cars are still whizzing by, but none of that can be heard.

Ruben blinks, and a calm comes over his face. He looks up to the sun all bright and beaming with light that ricochets through leaves on trees. Ruben's eyes release the tension they once held. His lips relax.

The scene continues without sound.

The screen fades to black.

It goes without saying, he made peace with silence.[1]

⸺

I do not know what sounds rise in your silence. I do not know what the lies tell or how they taunt you. I do not know what swells at the surface when you sit in still rooms or on couches that once held the frames of close companions. I do not know how hard it is to sit in car rides when it is you and only you. I do not know what is impossible about the stillness, if it is that your hands need things to do, or if it is that your racing thoughts rage—even with the medicine, even with the verses memorized.

I do not know who once told you that your sitting still was not good enough. I do not know how you've come to believe that you move too much or speak too much or think too much to do a thing like *be still*.

But, like Ruben, it is time to learn that you *can* be still.

And it is time to accept that the silence *will* be good.

Sometimes, silence comes as a season without actual sound. Sometimes, silence comes as a season of slowness, simplicity, and going unseen. Sometimes, it is like a fallow field that seems to be withering, waiting, and wasting away.

The bad that you believed about silence—about seasons of slowness, simplicity, and being unseen—cannot be brought with you on this journey. It is time to unlearn the lies and embrace the truth. *Silence is good.* Silence can bring deep peace. Silence gives way to growth. It is generative, and there is always something going on under the surface of the soil.

Your seasons of silence—the ones that have gone and the ones that will come—are not death sentences. They are hardly even endings. In fact, the work of all seeds begins under the soil of the deep earth, where all is kept quiet.

There is a farming practice that consists of resting fields for the sake of regenerating them. It is an ancient concept, a biblical one, really. It's the practice of fallowing land—of breaking up the ground after it's been harvested from, then leaving it to lay and rest for a season.

This practice of fallowing land can ultimately lead to flourishing. Left to rest, fallow land has a chance to recover from the depletion that occurs after demanding seasons of farming. It is a slow, intentional season of leaving land to go unused and untouched. You can imagine what our consumeristic culture thinks about this unhurried, farm-to-table process.

As time goes on, so increases the appetite for food to come faster and cheaper. Deemed as too slow, too still, too long-drawn-out by consumers, this practice of fallowing land has been substantially abandoned.

Through the years, some farmers have resorted to using heavy machinery to quickly work the land. They've turned to using chemicals to promise "pest-free" produce. And, what most of us don't know is that instead of resting the land, they've come to overwork and overuse it, farming the same fields with no break.

On the surface, the world seemingly gets what it wants. Food that is fast, abundant, and cheap. But below the ground, the land is dying. It's losing its richness, its nutrients, its organic composition, all of which allow the harvest to flourish.

We are running the earth to death because we want to *do* and *have* and *eat* more.

We are running ourselves to death because we want to *do* and *have* and *be* more.

In an excerpt from one of my favorite books *Anonymous*, Alicia Britt Chole writes:

> When growth pauses, the trees have often become my teachers.
>
> What the plenty of summer hides, the nakedness of winter reveals: infrastructure. Fullness often distracts from foundations. But in the stillness of winter, the trees' true strength is unveiled. Stripped of decoration, the tree trunks become prominent.
>
> As a child I always colored tree trunks brown, but to my adult eyes they appear to be more of a warm gray. Starting with their thick bases, I begin studying each tree. Buckling strips of bark clothe mile after mile of weathered branches. Leafless, the trees feature their intricate support systems. Detail is visible, as is dead wood. Lifeless limbs concealed by summer's boasting are now exposed.
>
> My eyes glide from one rough, uneven bough to another and then to the terminal, delicate twigs. A tree's posture is all-open, like arms ready for an embrace. So very vulnerable, yet so very strong. I find the display quieting and full of grace.
>
> In winter, are the trees bare? Yes.
>
> In winter, are the trees barren? No.
>
> Life still is.
>
> Life does not sleep—though in winter she retracts all advertisement. And when she does so, she is conserving and preparing for the future.
>
> And so it is with us. Seasonally, we too are stripped of visible fruit. Our giftings are hidden; our abilities are underestimated. When previous successes fade and current efforts falter, we can easily mistake our fruitlessness for failure.
>
> But such is the rhythm of spiritual life: new growth, fruitfulness, transition, rest . . . new growth, fruitfulness, transition,

rest. Abundance may make us feel more productive, but perhaps emptiness has greater power to strengthen our souls.[2]

My friend Christine Marie Bailey, author of *The Kindred Life*, farms on seventeen acres of land in Sante Fe, Tennessee. She and her husband are sustainable farmers. This means that they farm for the sake of yielding produce, but they also farm for the sake of restoring the land. They cultivate their land, not just for the here and now but for all future seasons.

I asked Christine if she lets the fields on her farm go fallow.

Together, she and her husband rotate their crops, which is a way of allowing certain fields to rest while others work. She told me that, in addition to rest, they give their crops extra minerals and nutrients so that *as* they rest they can be deeply and richly restored.

Today, farmers have been seeing the generational impact of running their fields ragged. They are seeing how, in the here and now, overfarming easily supplies consumeristic demand. But the fields cannot and will not keep up this way. And farmers no longer want to rush and force food from the fields without any care for flourishing futures.

The earth is tired.
The land needs rest.

Let it lie, this fallow ground.
Let it rest.
This season is not wasted, no. The nutrients are
    sinking deep, replenishing what is needed to grow.
    Replenishing what was once stripped.
This season is not wasted, no.

What may appear barren or a wasteland is simply
     space—resting.
This fallow ground is resting, reminding you that rest
     is equally as important as the seasons of sowing,
     pruning and harvesting.

                                    —Mia Arrington

You are not a farm, and you are not a field. But you are a creating human, and the earth of your body is tired; the land in your life needs rest.

You do not always have to create. You do not always have to conjure up creative ideas and paintings and poems and posts. You can enjoy the art of others; you can partake in pieces formed by other human hands. You can look at paintings and simply stand in awe. You can break from bringing forth; you can pause from producing.

You can bring your hands and your body and your brain to slowness.

Stillness.

Silence.

Watching and waiting in the silence and in the unseen can be a beautiful process. It can be restful and restorative. You do not always have to make and muster up all there is.

You can rest from the work that remains within you.

You can rest from the work that remains within this world.

⸻

Our lives are no different from the land—we are tired, and we are depleted. We are overstimulated, and we are never still. We are noisy, and we neglect the silence. We are run-down, and we need restoration.

We are overfarmed, like fields with never-ending demands. Demands to do and be and give and create more. To know and hear more. To help more. To show up and serve more. To lead more. To experience more.

We produce and produce. We teach and tell. We create and curate. We pastor and we preach. We are tired and we fuel ourselves with coffee just to keep up with all the ways in which the world needs us.

Seasons of stillness come to us in different ways, in different seasons, and for different reasons. Sometimes they come to us by choice. Pastors who take sabbaticals, mothers on maternity leave, workers on vacation. Sometimes they come to us by chance.

Illness.

Loss.

Change.

Death.

You might not always summon your slow, silent seasons. You might not always wish for the pause or unproductivity. You might not ever ask for the change, or the crippling illness, or the lingering loss. You might not ever wish these seasons upon yourself.

Still, here they are.

And you cannot rush them away, just like you cannot wish or will winter away. You cannot pretend they are not present. You cannot dress them up in decorations or disguise. You can only live them. Greet them. Grieve them.

Walk through them.

Wait through them.

Renita J. Weems, minister and writer, writes:

Just as there are seasons of the year, there are seasons of the soul, changes in the atmospheric pressure that sweep over the human spirit. We move in and out of them, often without being aware of them, almost unconsciously, and frequently without appreciation for the new experiences they bring our way. Where does one begin talking about the dips and curves along the spiritual journey? How does a minister admit that she's been left slumping toward mystery more than she has been grasping mystery? What lessons have pulled me through? What happened to all those prayers I prayed and the ones I gave up praying along the way? It seems always that the task before me was learning how to distinguish when it was God who seemed hidden and when it was I who was hiding, and above all, learning how to wait out the time until we found our way back to each other.[3]

We press into silent seasons like a seed pressing into the soil. Jennifer Dukes Lee writes about pressing seeds "deep down, knowing that new life starts in dark, unseen places." This is where and when the story gets good, she says. "In the moment before the miracle . . . the moment of breakthrough."[4]

It just might be that you are in the silent season you never knew you needed. The retraction, the hiddenness, the broken ground, the waiting, the dark. This slow, unseen work that is done in the dark will yield new wonders and life in time. On the other side of this, there will be roots and stems and beauty and blooms. But for now, it is okay to sit with the silence and stillness.

> Did you know you could sit with grief,
> And not have to find immediate relief,
> Based on someone else's belief,
> That you shouldn't feel it at all?
>
> Did you know it's okay to rest,
> Like newborn babe at mama's breast,

Against the Giver of Life be pressed,
And all else you can forestall?

Did you know that Grace can grow,
In the hidden spaces that no one else knows,
And there's no one else that you have to show,
As you respond to His healing call?

Did you know that which fills the soul up,
Is what will soon overflow that soul's cup,
And all you need do is be still and sup,
At the table prepared by the Lord of all?

—Bethany Robin Biter

The slow, silent, and unseen place you are in is good. It is a healing space; it is a hope-filled space. In this quiet time of respite, take inventory of where and how you feel depleted. Ask yourself honest questions and look at the work you put your hands to.

Where is there burnout?

Where is there striving?

Where is there overextension?

Where is there exhaustion?

As you locate these places, may you nourish yourself with the nutrients you need. Fill up on the things that restore and revive you. This will heal you for the here and now, but it will also prepare you for the future work you will do. Surround yourself with books, encouraging people, mentors of the creative passions you've paused from pursuing.

There is purpose in this process, and there is so much unseen life in this silent season. It might be hard to hear and hard to believe.

It *is* hidden; nevertheless, it is here.

Prayer

God, quiet my soul and quiet my mind. Open my ears to hear that you are always speaking. Open my eyes to see that you are always moving and working. You are creating new life in and through me, even when the work of my hands comes to a pause. Thank you for the goodness that grows beneath the surface. Thank you for loving and leading me through all my seasons. Amen.

Prompts

How is silence or stillness hard for you?
How is silence or stillness healing for you?

Practices

Take a trip and travel to a place where you can rest from your making and producing. A cabin in the woods. A mountain house with no internet connection. A beach house with only the bare necessities. Put yourself in positions and places where you must intentionally embrace silence and stillness.

Read books. Reading is restful, simply for the fact that it invites you to relish in the created work of another. Let *leisurely* reading be the nourishment that you need in slow and unseen seasons.

Pieces

I've spent my whole adult life trying to outgrow this shell of quiet that has defined me. A world perplexed by the observant stillness of my character questions, "Why don't you talk more?" My mind races, "Do my thoughts have no value unless I give birth to them in speech? Do they find me dimwitted? Speech is a currency I do not possess. But goodness, I have grand dreams and bold opinions and poetic musings. These are not the topics they seek, though. See, I know this question. It is born of insecurity and judgement of their own unquietness. In a world that can't keep quiet, my quiet nature is peculiar. Because if they were prodded to stillness, they'd be forced to confront all the thoughts they avoid." With this realization, I smile knowingly and without a word, disappear into the crowd.

—Ashley Woods

When life becomes stressful, when heavy things weigh on me, when grief needs its space, the quiet helps keep me from being consumed by overwhelm. The more I find quiet stillness and learn to listen, the more the noises around me sound like a beautiful symphony and less like clanging cymbals that make me want to press my hands over my ears and tune out. Quieting helps me tune in. Quieting helps me center on the One whose voice I long to hear loudest. Quieting helps me breathe and find presence in the moment.

—Kristin Vanderlip

Let There Be Thought

Imagination gives us wings to create.

—Makoto Fujimura, *Art + Faith:*
A Theology of Making

I remember going to an amusement park as a kid and pausing in the middle of all my fun to look up at the sky and scale the roller coasters spinning wild. I remember thinking about children in other places of the world. I wondered if, wherever they were, they'd had roller coasters too and could ride them for sheer fun, for sheer pleasure.

Six Flags.

I do not remember my age, but I remember my thoughts, the way I wondered how people like my oldest brother, earthbound in wheelchairs, might have felt when they found out they could not ride the roller coasters or take the stairs up to the Drop of Doom and scream the whole one hundred stories down.

As a kid, I was always contemplating big and deep thoughts on fairness and on equality, thoughts on danger, and especially thoughts on death.

My thoughts on death rippled like the shallows. Insubstantially deep, at first, then crashing in closer, like billowing waves on the shoreline. I think deeply; I drive myself into a limbo, like rockets in outer space suspended against an endless horizon of questions and curiosities.

How does a baby feel when it's born? How does a star know how to shine? Do trees whisper with their leaves? What does it feel like when we die?

It's always an endless taunting of wonderings.

Is eternity life after death; is it a place? Is it time? Is it a place *in* time, or a place *without* time? Is it a space in the sky that swallows up all the souls saved by God?

How does it work?

How do we go?

Where do we go?

Why do we go?

I know I am not alone in this, alone in the wandering and wading of wild waters, the thinking about how life works. I know I am not alone in my wanting to sit down with God over coffee and pancakes—or whatever it is that he eats and drinks—and cut straight through the small talk to get to the sure, concrete answers.

If you're a thinker, I'm sure there is an ocean of riptides pushing and pulling at you too. Thoughts so deep and unresolved, you've stopped entertaining them for fear you'll drown and never make it back to the water's surface.

And so, there in the shallows you've been. Where it is calm and where the water brushes gently. Where you do not have to swim far or sink deep. Where you do not have to choose between things, where you barely have to believe in any one thing. In the shallows is most likely where you keep your faith. Where you don't have to worry about your boat rocking or your so-called "unbelief" dragging you out into the deep.

The shorelines, that's where you are tied up and anchored. *Land ahoy*, your nautical vow to never leave the land you stand on, the land you're safe on.

Except, there is a world of wonder beyond the shallows. It is a world of daunting mystery, *yes*. But you do not have to be afraid of the rise and fall of waves, of the salt water washing cool and cold over you. You can sail off into that great, wide, vast ocean. With all of its mystery beneath you. You can release your keeping heart from its fear of the deep, from its fear of the thoughts that rise within.

You can contemplate, ruminate, think, question, brood, and ponder. You can dare to see and dare to dream beyond the boundary of these brushing waves.

You, with that magnificent mind, just might be the kind of art-filled soul that has the courage to really see.

You are an asker of questions.

You are a creative visionary.

Your art is your ideas.

Your art is *you*.

One of my favorite things about Jesus is the fact that he is strategic, the fact that his coming in the flesh was the result of a plan that came from a word set forth since the beginning of time.

The first time I realized this was when I read *The Master Plan of Evangelism* by Robert E. Coleman. You'll yawn just by taking one look at the cover. But I mean it when I say that the book will breathe new life into your beliefs about God. It's changed my life, having learned that our artfully *creative* God is also a strategically *calculated* God.

> It all started by Jesus calling a few men to follow him. This revealed immediately the direction his evangelistic *strategy* would take. His concern was not with the programs to reach the multitudes, but with men whom the multitudes would follow.[1]

We always say Jesus came for the masses. We always say he came for the many and for the multitudes. But the thing we rarely talk about and the thing we rarely teach is that, *really*, Jesus came for a small number of men and women. *He came for the few.*

Jesus knew that his time on earth would be short. He memorized his mission; he understood his assignment. He knew what God's plan was and therefore knew what his *purpose* was.

Yes . . . Jesus's heart was for healing and helping the masses.

But his ultimate *purpose* was the cross. His ultimate *purpose* was forgiveness. His ultimate *purpose* was saving souls from eternal damnation. His ultimate *purpose* was to spiritually rescue *all*. This is why his *focus* was on the *few*. He strategically came to intentionally invest in a small number of men and women who would surround and support him on this mission.

He privately, even painfully, knew that this strategy would best spread the message of salvation far and wide. The epitome of his ministry wasn't merely healing disease and casting out demons—it was discipleship.

It was always discipleship; it will always be discipleship.

The art of discipleship is that it's the math of the kingdom. It's about numbers and logic and investment and strategy. It's about multiplication—the one teaching the twelve, the twelve preaching to the crowds, the crowds gathering in masses, the masses proclaiming the message to *all* the world.

The compassion of Jesus is that he healed who he could. He performed as many miracles as he could while remaining focused on his mission—his time with a few, his life for all.

I sometimes wonder how Jesus felt knowing something that no one else knew, seeing a vision that no one else saw. I wonder how he lived through the loneliness, how he carried a burden so heavy and deep. I wonder how misunderstood he felt in those moments when he chose between serving or saying no to the crowd.

When I think about this, I fall in love with Jesus all over again. Because, honestly, while we default to seeing the greatness of his love on the cross, I can't help but believe that we can also see the magnitude of his love in the miracles he never made happen.

It's in the moments Jesus stepped *away* from the masses, away from the glaring needs of the obvious for the sake of focusing on his ministry with the few—a plan that would someday unravel his mission for all.

Your uncompromising vision that bubbles under the surface, your unapologetic strategy—your master plans, ideas, questions, curiosities, notions, schemes, dreams, logic, and reason—are all signs of compassionate creativity.

Creativity doesn't require that you paint or dance or sing about what is beautiful. You can think, fixate on, analyze, and strategize about what is better.

This is art too.

My friend Morgan Harper Nichols writes about the idea of the "Mountain of Mind," in her book *Forty Days on Being a Five*. About those of us who tend to dwell in our minds, she writes:

> We do not have to be everywhere doing everything at once, and, perhaps, deep within, we know this. When we start to learn that our ability to conceptualize and look at things objectively can actually be the way we begin to let go of things, we move from detachment to non-attachment. We move from staying away from others and keeping them at a distance to bringing what we learned at a distance into the present moment—with others, in community, in the world. We come down from the *mountain of mind* back down to earth and share what we have found.[2]

On my blog, I wrote about Morgan's words and how they make me feel like I am looking into a mirror and being soothed to confess the truth of how I am. Her words bring me to think about L'Engle and the way in which physics inspired her works of fiction. It moves my soul to think that beautiful, imaginative stories like *A Wrinkle in Time* were born partly because of their basis in science—a field that is scantily seen for the beauty it, too, possesses.[3]

It is the *thinkers* who forge ahead into foreign territories. It is the scientists, doctors, mathematicians, and philosophers who creatively solve problems and pioneer new paths of understanding, invention, and discovery. And there is a whole world of us out here. We are the ones using imagination and intellect to form formulas and study the sciences. We are the ones analyzing and hypothesizing better ways for our world.

We are the ones inspiring people because we incubate ideas.
We are the ones loving deeply because we think deeply.
We are the ones shining light because we peer into the dark.
And we have believed that we are not creative. Believed that if it is not pretty paint on canvas, or clay spinning wild into stunning shapes, that it is not beautiful in its offering. That it is not imaginative or innovative or artfully attractive. Makoto Fujimura, artist and founder of the International Arts Movement (IAM), writes:

> The arts in some ways are fundamental to even scientific research and mathematics. We talk about needing math and science education all the time, but we don't realize that they start with an intuitive process. Mathematics is not just this mechanism that you teach, but true math is this creative process of re-examining these abstract concepts and not making things up. They are grounded in reality, but they have these margins that you question deeply, even the assumptions that these abstractions are really giving you. And so at the core level, all the disciplines need to have a grasp on the intuitive side of our experiential side.[4]

It is beyond time for daring to see the domains of reason, logic, science, and math for the beauty they behold and the creative opportunities that they produce. It's time to see analytical, visionary, and intellectual skills for the life-changing contributions they make in and for our world.

Your contemplation counts for creativity. Your thinking, all the ways in which you retract to reflect; your silent presence in the pews at the back of the church where you ruminate on the ways we can love and lead better; the unseen years spent in consideration of the book you feel you were born to write;

even the ideas that are only in your head, even if your plans and purpose remain unexpressed for now—all of this counts for creativity.

All of this counts for the way you care.

And you do not have to be afraid that you will be swept up in wonder. You do not have to fear that you will drown in the depths of your waves and ways.

If you can believe in the truth of a God great enough to create a world of galaxies, then you can believe in the truth of a God great enough to cradle the world of *your* intricacies, theories, and curiosities.

Prayer

God, teach me how to unlearn the lies I've come to believe about myself. Let me see the ways you made me. Let me learn the ways you love me. As I ponder your mysteries, help me lead the world to see your light. Unravel my understanding with your unfathomable love. Help me lead others to your great truth. Dazzle me with your vastness. Inspire my ideas. Amen.

Prompts

What are your wonderings about the galaxies?
What are your wonderings about your own intricacies?

Practices

Take a drive and ruminate with instrumental music in the background. Give yourself permission to think. Write out your thoughts in a journal, record them on your phone, scratch them out on a big chalkboard. Let the expression of these thoughts and theologies and theories remind you that your thoughts matter. Your logic and reasoning and innovative inquiries cannot only change you from within, but they can change the world.

Deviate from fiction and read a book on science, mathematics, or theology. Let your mind fly in a field that it finds interest in. Explore a theory, a concept, or a subject of study that you know nothing about. Share your revelations with friends and fellow creatives.

Pieces

People mistake introversion for weakness.
We are thinkers.
We hold our words until they have power.
We mean what we say, even if we don't speak often.
We love one-on-one connection over crowds, because
    we want to absorb what you are sharing with us.
We often marry extroverts, because they bring us joy,
    and we bring them peace (a beautiful exchange).
We retreat to energize ourselves, because our deep
    processing happens on the inside.
You'll find us in corners.
On sidelines.
At the back of the room.

But we are not weak.
No, do not be mistaken.
We are leaders, too.

> —Faith Cole

Emerge. Something everyone notices. We see what comes out.
We praise and critique the emergence. The celebratory activity
or debilitating words of defeat carry so much weight. We tend
to forget that in order for something to rise up there had to be
some immense work below the surface.

> —Harry Walls IV

Let There Be Fellowship

> Long Years apart—can make no
> Breach a second cannot fill—
> The absence of the Witch does not
> Invalidate the spell—
>
> The embers of a Thousand Years
> Uncovered by the Hand
> That fondled them when they were Fire
> Will stir and understand—
>
> > —Emily Dickinson,
> > "Long Years apart—can make no"

There is always a quest—some grandiose need to save the world from flying dragons and wicked wizards, from the hearts of men who have risen in power and will not, for the sake of the war-torn world, relent.

It's always a quest to calm the fires wreaking havoc on weak villages, a quest to loosen the laws of lords who have ruined the land with famine and war. And there is always a hero, and the hero is brave and usually has no choice but to bear the burden they were (as fate would have it) born with. And there is this one and only truth that will never change for the hero, no matter the setting, no matter the story. And that is that the hero never goes alone—they never fight alone, and they never win alone.

My leather couch.

Of course, I am on the couch, because it would only be right for me to write about fellowship after having watched *The Fellowship of the Ring* for the umpteenth time. I cannot get the Council of Elrond out of my head, the scene where Elrond speaks:

> Strangers from distant lands. Friends of old. You've been summoned here to answer the threat of Mordor. Middle-earth stands upon the brink of destruction. None can escape it. You will unite or you will fall. Each race is bound to this fate, this one doom.[1]

I cannot type, and I'm sure that you cannot read, those words without chills traveling down the spine, for it is a gut-wrenching, heart-stopping display of fellowship, of slow-fostered friendship. But it is not the only scene or the only story that displays the miracle of friendships bound together by fight and fate. It's also Charlie Bucket and Grandpa Joe,[2] it is Sherlock Holmes and Dr. Watson,[3] it is Iron Man and the Avengers,[4] it is Robin Hood and Little John.[5]

And it is also *you*, the human and the hero learning to link arms with the ones you love, the ones you lead with. And I have no fear in confessing that this has been the hardest chapter to write, because fellowship, as it always seems, is the hardest chapter in life.

We lose friends just as soon as we learn to love them. We move and we make new ones. We are broken by them and we break them ourselves.

I almost wish that Elrond's words read differently. I almost wish he'd said, *You will unite and you will also fall*, for I am finding that falling in friendship is inevitable—it is not apart from the journey, it is a part of it.

I sometimes wonder if God, looking deep into our hearts, sees a mosaic of messy pieces, our sharp shards and jagged edges all brilliantly placed together, piece by shattered piece. I wonder if it was always his plan to bring us all together, to make a melded masterpiece that tells the miraculous story of men and women coming to find that there's more than just a glimpse of good in this world. That there is gold—that shimmering shade of refined, requited love.

We need community and, deeper still, we need *creative* community. We need to be reminded that our hearts, our art, all pine to point toward a greater purpose. We need to be reminded that we are welcome as we are, that we are welcome for *all* we are, all blood and bone and burdens and brokenness. We need to be reminded that we are wanted for who we are, not what we do or produce or can prove.

I will always be fascinated by the friendship between C. S. Lewis and Tolkien. I will always be captivated by the commitment they shared to each other's words, to each other's worlds. Sometime before the pandemic I went with my friend Suzy to see, for the second time in my life, *The Screwtape Letters*, presented by Fellowship for Performing Arts at the Belk Theater at Blumenthal Performing Arts Center.

At the end of the performance, the crew took the time to answer questions from the audience. Someone asked about the reception of *The Screwtape Letters*, which Lewis wrote as a fictional work of satire. The crew shared that while the book was and is still widely received, there is one person who was known for *not* being fond of the work. This person believed Lewis's decision to pit Satan as "good" against the Christian as "bad" to be a questionable, confusing approach.

Who did this opinion belong to?

It was Tolkien himself, one of Lewis's closest companions.[6]

Even still, their friendship flourished. Though they disagreed, though their work was different, it turns out the most compelling thing about the legacy of their friendship is not only that they cared for each other but that they cared for each other's work.

———

One thing I hear often from writers, artists, and people who long to create is that they worry there is already someone out there in the world writing what they want to write, making what they want to make.

They say *the books have all been written* and *the best ideas for businesses already belong to someone else*. They say that all of what is "out there" is bigger and better than what they could ever come up with and create.

But I cannot for the life of me let go of how, for present-day believers in Christ, the practice of our faith is hinged upon a book that contains four different epistles by four different authors all writing about the same thing.

The coexistence of these letters does not lessen their witness, it strengthens it. The letters do not compete with one another, they complement each other. They provide confirmation and cross-references for one another. They legitimize and justify each other.

Creativity is commonplace; it is a shared characteristic that runs through our lives. There isn't a faction of chosen individuals who are the only ones meant and made to carry this thing out. Our contributions are a melding of many voices in many mediums.

We can create and not compete.

We make alongside of friends.

We can tell the same stories in different ways.

We can tell different stories and want the same things.

L'Engle writes about this in *Walking on Water* when she quotes Jean Rhys:

> All of writing is a huge lake. There are great rivers that feed the lake, like Tolstoy and Dostoyevsky. And there are mere trickles, like Jean Rhys. All that matters is feeding the lake. I don't matter. The lake matters. You must keep feeding the lake.[7]

In our writing and in our making, in all creative contributions, we are feeding the lake. We are answering the call to save Middle-earth, we are on that grandiose quest to save a war-torn world.[8]

And it is not you and Katniss Everdeen;[9] it is not you and Sherlock Holmes.[10] It is you and the friends *you* have and hold in the flesh. It is the whole cowardly team of you with all your failures and your flaws, all your worries and all your weaknesses.

It's Meredith and me, sitting across from each other at a main street cafe. Her long, brown hair and eyes of gold, her gentle voice telling me dreams for the words she's working on, dreams for the words that are working in her.

It's Angel and the way she laughs so beautifully, poetically. It's the way wisdom drips from her lips, the way it spins truth into song.

It's Renee, reading words to me from her journal. It's her speaking aloud the stories of her unshakeable faith, as we rock on the waves of our beautiful lake.

It's Courtney, and the fire in her eyes. The strength of the fight in her voice that cries out in song for the ones her heart holds.

It's Mia, Sarah, Katie, Jazmine, Tiffany, Lamar, and Harry sending swells of messages as we forge our way forward in creativity.

It's Beth, the artisans, and everyone I love at BraveWorks, coming together through community and creativity. It's their courage that compelled me to craft this manifesto, inspired by the artisans these words are about:

My hands are capable and my future is bright. I am coming to courage and I am finding the light. There is joy to grow and there is joy to give. I am building anew and beginning again. Transformed beyond the surface, I will heal from pain to purpose. Stitch by stitch, bead by bead, day by day—I am becoming brave.

It's my (in)courage sisters and the way their written words find a way to work grace through the darkest corners of my heart.

It's my grandma when she teaches me to say *I am woman. Hear me roar.* It's my mom when she tells me her dreams of building businesses to better this broken world. It's my dad when he sends me pictures of his garden, his hands holding out for hope in the here and now.

166

It's flashbacks of my brothers and me and the way our imaginations made way for play. It's memories that will never fade, even as we change and age.

It's childhood memories of cousins who always felt more like brothers and sisters. It's the shared grief in our eyes over lost loved ones. It's the glimmer in our hearts that says we're still here and we can't give up now.

I need these friends; I need this family. I need their loving lungs breathing life into mine. I even need them beyond what I need *from* them. I need them to keep being who they are for the sake of what they offer the world. I need the witness of their living to keep reminding me that we're all here needing the same thing.

We're all here for and by love.

It's childhood memories of cousins who always felt more

This book, this very spine in your hands, is the result of community. It is not the result of a solo act; it is the sum of the people and places I've come to know and love. This book is the result of the people and places that have poured into me, whether they realized it or not.

Every home I stepped foot into. Every hug that held my hurting hands. Every prayer circle welcoming me to pour out my heart. Every home-cooked meal. Every holiday spent with family. Every laugh shared with long-lost friends. Every small group leader who helped me learn about life—all the Kivians and Marias, all the Annies, Dawns, and Paulas. Every back and forth with Emma over email. Every card sent by Kaye.

It's Joanne walking through the snowstorm to visit me in the delivery room. It's Jess and me writing songs with our guitars.

These memories, these moments, these people, and these places have been burned into my being, singed into my soul.

And they have refined the impurities of my character, called me out to love, and led me into the light where I belong.

It is the most liberating, exhilarating thing to confess that something you forged and fashioned—something, like this book, that you gave birth to and breathed life into—came into being not because of *you* but because of all that is a part of you.

The line from a movie that inspired your poem. The song that moved you to dance inside your home. The written words of your friend and how they compelled you to write your own.

Like my friend Courtney Turner who, after reading a poem I posted on Instagram, responded by writing a poem of her own. Of the words I wrote about my health and hurting heart, *she* wrote:

> Mercy met me where my anger swelled.
> Grace covered me where my sadness dwells.
> Jesus held me right where I fell.
> My body fails, but He never will.

This is fellowship.

In the fight of life you find friends to walk beside you. To cheer you on and challenge you. To see you, know you, and need you too.

It's only fitting that along with this call to fellowship, I talk about peer critique—which is just a fancy way of saying creative community. It was in my Writing Theory class at Nyack College where I first realized that peer critique is a sacred act of community and conversation. It holds the potential to center people together, despite their differences.

Peter Elbow, Professor of English Emeritus at the University of Massachusetts, is a pioneer of freewriting as well as writing practices that promote the decentering of teachers. My own thoughts and theories on writing—on the egalitarian nature of it, the need for seeing the writing and editing processes as separate, the power of writing, and the powerful process of peer critique—have been widely and deeply formed by the pedagogies of Peter Elbow. Elbow speaks of the feedback process as being like a "group of amateur musicians who get together once a week to play for each other's enjoyment." He writes:

> In fact I think that the fear of honest feedback is not so much a fear that the other person will think us wrong, childish, evil, or stupid. Those are easy to take in comparison with our worst fear: that our words were not heard at all.[11]

I wonder if that's true for you, like it once was for me. If I told you that the very thing you need for your creativity is *community*, would you believe me? Would you believe that there really are safe people and places in which you can and should release the truth of your words, the work the world requires of you?

Like Samwise Gamgee, walking with his friend Frodo Baggins to the top of Mount Doom in Mordor. Tired, tried, and tempted, Frodo tells Sam that he can't do it; he won't make it as the ring of power weighs on his soul.

"I can't carry it for you," Sam says. "But I can carry you!"[12]

This is fellowship.

That we might carry, and be carried, in our creativity.

Prayer

God, I inhale grief, I exhale goodness. I confess broken community; I confess failed friendships. I proclaim my belief in the possibility of fellowship. I turn my eyes to look toward the sun. I believe in the dawn of a new day. Soften my heart and strengthen my hope. Remind me that I do not walk alone. Call me out to carry the burdens of the ones I love and to trust that they can do the same for me. Amen.

Prompts

Fiction: How would you and your friends save the world?
Nonfiction: How are you and your friends saving the world?

Practices

Hold a firepit of fellowship with committed creatives or close friends. Invite them into a time of peer critiquing. Foster friendships off-line and behind the scenes. Welcome friendship in your real world and your creative world. Show your art and work before it is done. Let close companions have a say to speak into it, and into you.

Join a creative community, like Fallow Ink, to connect with others who are walking the same path as you. Join for the sake of engagement, encouragement, critique, learning, and leadership. Above all, strive to seek out friendships, whether virtual or face-to-face. You will fall and things will fail, but you will find unity and it will be worth it.

Pieces

There was a time when
the news came on at five
and books were sold in stores
and notes were written by hand
and the grocers knew your name
and children played outside
and food was prepared in kitchens
and phones were attached to walls
and porches were for people
not
packages.

> —Ashley Whittemore

If it's Sunday, and the place is packed,
Then I better hear musical sounds.
   If rhythms compel my knees to
dance,
   Then my soul knows that I'm free,
free, free.
   If quiet melodies are whispered,
Then in serenity, I will pray.
If I am challenged and encouraged,
Then this church is what I will call home.
Cue the praise break, cue the call to prayer.

If you see me singing and dancing,
Then I pray you'll sing and dance with me.
If you respect and hear my story,
Then we'll slowly spirit'ally heal.
   If you sense beauty in many forms,

Then celebrate all forms of devotion.
Cue the praise break, cue the call to prayer.

   If we can talk with both souls at
peace,
Then we can fellowship together.
   If we both express our faith freely,
Then the Spirit of David is here.
If we can be hopeful through
goodness,
   If we can be hopeful through
   lamentation,
   Then we will have found the
meaning of joy,
The meaning of unity,
The meaning of the nest of my faith and fellowship.
Cue the praise break, cue the call to prayer

                              —Medomfo Owusu

14

Let There Be Remembrance

You get a feeling when you look back on life that that's all God really wants from us, to live inside a body he made and enjoy the story.

—Donald Miller, *A Million Miles in a Thousand Years*

This is the part where I rip my heart wide open, invite you deep in the farthest corner, sit you down and tell you about how we lost him to COVID-19, lost him because his body was broken and it was time to let it lay in rest. Lost him because his lungs could no longer pump breath to the blood beneath his beautiful bronze skin. We lost his body but not his burning love, that kind of love that brought him with bags of groceries to the back doors of our homes.

On Zoom.

I will begin with his silver hair, and the way it dazzled and shone, and the freckles on his face and how I could not have counted them all, even if I tried. There were his tinkering hands and how they were always fixing, always finding cars to repair or doorknobs to replace. Hands that took to the handle of a shed that never held enough tools. Hands that softly touched the backs of every one of us as he whispered prayer and blessing into thin air.

I will tell you about that broad nose, the telltale sign of a Black man, and the furrow of his brow bent with Native pride. And I will never forget those lips, and how they burned with one thousand bedtime stories about first homes and the cost of bread, about life growing up and knowing God, about the many men and women he met along the way.

I will tell you how I miss him and how his death left a hole right here in the middle of my heart. But I am becoming okay, coming to peace, because I am coming to remembrance. I am coming to find the trail of tales he left with a legacy that will long outlast his breath, so much so that it feels like he is still here with me, with all of us.

I will tell you how, just a few weeks after his passing, I stood in my bathroom staring into a mirror stained with specks of toothpaste spit. I fixed my hair, pulled it behind my ears, and made my face up with all the chemicals, creams, and colors. Then I took a brush to my son's hair, long curls of auburn red just like my own. I told him we were dressing up even though we weren't leaving the house, even though we were only going to turn on the computer and sit in our dining chairs to watch the virtual viewing of Pop, the one who lost life to the faint pushing of breath in his lungs.

When we lost him, I was eight months round and in the swell of pregnancy with my second son. When we lost him, the world was in the swell of a high wave of rising COVID-19 cases, loved ones losing life left and right.

I watched the viewing as the wobbly camera captured my family speaking words of remembrance and sprinkling flowers atop my grandfather's grave. I watched the snow on the burial grounds glisten as it lit up under the sun, reflecting right on through my computer screen. I could almost feel the chill of New York's bitter air as much as I felt the warm tears rolling down my cheeks, crying muted into the camera.

The tears came because there was sorrow, but the tears also came because there was hope. As I sat there, cradling life in one hand and death in the other, I listened to the story of my grandfather's last moments, how he pointed to the ceiling of that hospital room and motioned to his three children that he was ready to be home, really *home*.

While I watched, I did not feel a sting or a burning anger or that raging need-to-know of why and how. I did not see a body swallowed up by dirt and death. Instead, I saw hope rise as I reflected on the life of a man who had lived a life of love.

A man who lived a good story.

A man who *told* good stories.[1]

I did not know then—did not know as a young girl in the back seat of Pop's car riding to and from church in his gold Saturn sedan—that he would come to be the greatest story-teller I'd ever know. I didn't know then how his stories were undoubtedly the most annoying thing to endure and yet the most *anointed* thing to endure.

The man could spin a story with any stranger he'd met on the street.

I didn't know it then, but he wasn't a mere man who talked too much; he was a man who told tales, a man who told stories as a way of stretching himself out to selflessly see and serve the people around him. He weaved comedy with tragedy, shared confessions about losing a son to leukemia, and made proclamations about the mysterious provisions of God. He could make a person laugh and cry all in the same breath, could make them come to see the inevitable goodness of God, whether they realized it or not, whether they believed it or not.

And the point of all of this is that, whether you realize it or not, you have stories that stir deep within you too. And if you are brave enough and believe enough that they are meaningful and that they matter, you just might save these stories. Give them breath enough that they cannot die with you when you leave this earth behind.

The stories will live on like legacies, lacing the very lives of the ones you lived to love.

This is because we do not simply listen to stories, we *live* them. Stories speak to people; they awaken the brain to see that there is a person in a place with a purpose coming up against a particular problem. Stories show us that, at one point or another, every person has the chance to persevere.

This is the way of God, that every one of us would see that we, too, are people in a place with a purpose coming up against the chance to persevere.

Our lives are stories lived within a greater story. Like paragraphs on the page, our lives make up the narrative of a grander novel. And it isn't just happening to you; it is happening *through* you.

The memories you are making will become stories you'll learn to live and tell. From that babbling baby looking up at you, to the stranger in the store you met five days ago—the stories you tell matter. They matter for now, and they matter for next year. They matter for you, and they matter for the generation coming *behind* you.

Your telling of them requires nothing from you—not a degree, not a paintbrush, not even pen and paper. Your telling requires nothing but the brave opening of your mouth, the brave sharing of what you know and believe to be true.

There is another way too.

Another way in which you do not need to fumble for words to say, do not need to open your mouth to speak. You do not have to be a storyteller to leave a legacy. You do not need to be an author or illustrator. You do not need to be like Maurice Sendak or Eric Carle.[2]

One of the most beautiful ways of leaving legacies of remembrance is through letters. Letters capture and memorialize a person within a time and place gone by.

I wish I could tell you the weight of my chest as I held my breath when I stepped into my grandfather's room the first time after he died. I wish I could tell you how tears welled within my eyes, stealing glances at his work shoes neatly kept beside the bed.

I wish I could tell you the precise sound of my silent sobbing, the sorrow and sighs I let seep out when my hands held the book that I never knew existed, the one with Pop's handwriting, filling in blank spaces between black lines, answering questions in a sort of *your story, your words* kind of book.

I wish I could tell you how I laughed through the burn of my tears when I finally deciphered his handwriting and read that one of his favorite songs growing up was "Satisfaction" by The Rolling Stones.

And, oh, the sizes in which my heart stretched that day, to read the words I'd always heard my grandfather pray—that the greatest desire of his life was for everyone in his family to know and love Jesus Christ.

Writing on pages will always be living proof of the legacies our loved ones leave behind. When minds fail and when memories fade, handwritten notes with hope-filled words will still remain.

And it goes two ways. Our loved ones can leave behind their letters and things. But we, too, can write words that lend way to their legacies. One way we do this is through writing obituaries.

Obituaries are stories that swell with remembrance. Here is a piece I wrote on Instagram, after I wrote Pop's obituary:

I spent the weekend writing an obituary. Not some bestselling novel. Or a song. Or a stunning poem. But an obituary. And while the tears gathered in my eyes and as I choked back my cry, it occurred to me that, sometimes, our words won't be the grandest. Sometimes, we need not spin sentences with heart-gripping stories. Not sit there, summoning magic and wonder and allure. Sometimes, we need only for our words to simply show up. Need only for our words to simply say, *plain and simply say*, that we fiercely saw and deeply loved the soul of another. It doesn't have to be a thriller, every time. Doesn't have to be a revelation, a message for the masses, a speech for seas of people, a soul-shattering sermon, an encore of a performance, a post gone viral, an award-winning anything. Write the letter. Send the email. Post on the private page. Fill the journal. Type the obituary. Let your words be small, let them sometimes be for the few eyes and small crowds that surround and see you. Sometimes, just sometimes, let your words be for only you and your people. And, in the smallest, slightest ways, you will watch as your words come to be a balm for the ones you love and cherish.

Your words will be a balm.
Your words will be a balm.
Your words will be a balm.

Your words can, *and will*, be a balm. Not just for this big, broken world. But for *your* world. That one that only your beating heart bears witness to.

After I wrote a tribute to Pop on my Instagram, my friend Kayla sent me a message with a poem of her own. She wrote:

I wanted to share this with you. I wrote it in my journal thinking of you and life. I finally got some thoughts on paper after being inspired by you. I'm not a writer but I love you and even though I'm no poet or author I feel like the fruits of your labor are people finding their ability to write even in small ways. So here you go:

Today I was thinking about snow. Snow and grief. I was sad the snow didn't stick, I was sad my dear friend lost someone she loved. Then I realized that snow is like grief. It can come and go in deafening flurries or in short pangs. It brings with it memories and emotions. It's a thing of days gone by, a signal that things die and start anew. What is so beautiful about this is right in that—we are reminded of days gone by, storms of emotion and memory. The pangs don't last forever. Just like snowflakes. They fall over us, cover the places they fall, on the ground and in our souls.

Then it's gone! Just like that!

Don't fret though. It's not really gone, the beautiful snow. The glorious grief that is filled with memories of what is lost. It'll come back and visit us when we are least expecting it. In the dead of the night it will find us. Resting over everything like a blanket of silence and thought. Reminding us once more of what was and that it won't always be. Hold onto the snow. Don't wish it away so fast. Let it linger, until it doesn't.

I am stunned and in awe of the impact of my post, a piece honoring the legacy of Pop, and how it inspired a poem to rise up and out of Kayla.

This is how and why legacy laces our lives with meaning, because it resonates the sacred experiences of our shared existence. This is what our words can do—what the stories, letters, sketches, photographs, and videos of our loved ones can do.

Listen for the stories.

Look for the ways in which we leave the witness of our love behind. The love notes and love letters, the captions of photographs and the scrapbooks.

In December 2019, just months before the COVID-19 pandemic began, I lost the sweetest soul who spoke a calm into the wild ways of my youth. Words don't often come quickly to me, but they do come deeply and surely. On January 4, 2020, over a week after my friend Halldis passed away, I finally wrote:

So many of us ride on the prayers of those that came before us. We ride on their faithfulness; we ride on the foundations they forged. And by ride, I mean soar. By ride, I mean fly. We grow deep and wide into the people we've always been destined to become mostly because of the souls that made sacrifices to shape and shift the world to turn its kind and gracious face towards us. Someday, someone will say the same of us. That we didn't labor in vain. That it all meant something. That every prayer offered, every scripture recited, every wordy and lengthy hymn sung meant something. But the pendulum pauses on this day—this year, this generation, this era—2020 when we will watch some of the bravest, purest, strongest souls pass from this life and into their next. Today, my soul gives thanks for the life of Halldis, a beautiful Norwegian woman who knew me as a six-year-old. Who hugged and loved frizzy-haired teenaged me. Who prayed for college-aged me. Who held the whining son of mom-aged me. Who told and told me time and again: "I'm praying for your future husband. Not just someone who is compatible, but someone who will complement you." Who listened to all of my long and drawn out stories and replied to every one of them with: "That's nice. Oh, that's really nice." Who believed in me because she believed God was for me, well before I understood belief myself. With tears as I write this, Halldis, your voice is branded in my brain. And when I sing about how great our God is, I will remember you, sweet sister.

Before the funeral, I spoke on the phone with my mom about Halldis's passing and the impossibility of me being home in New York to honor her life and say goodbye. I told my mom how I didn't want to send flowers that would soon fade and be forgotten. I told her how I couldn't just send a simple note because Halldis meant more to me than a Hallmark card.

"Write a poem," she said.

"A poem?" I asked.

She said that this was something I could do that would be endearing *and* enduring. So, I wrote:

Woven
Their wrinkled hands woven

Together tell of a love that knew no end
From the land they loved, to
the land they lived,
to start a family so filled,
a future found on faith.
The two became one,
then led the hundreds into holy union
with God himself.
Their beautiful lives woven,
together, a holy moment,
a holy memory.

About a year and a half later, Nils, Halldis's loving husband, passed away too. It was another virtual funeral for me, streaming live from my office and staring long into the screen.

Watching the livestream, there were familiar faces and voices scattered about singing songs and reading Scripture. There were testimonials filled with crying and bouts of comic relief.

Among the voices, I heard that of John Harris who pastored me through my teenage years. Pastor John, poised at the podium, spoke a truth that I won't soon forget.

"Long after the sermons," he said, "long after the alliterated points have been forgotten, his life and his legacy, they will continue to preach and they will continue to speak."

I wrote Pastor John's words down, knowing I'll someday repeat them and someday reuse them. I wrote them down, knowing I'll someday need to be reminded of them.

I wrote them down, knowing in my bones that they were true.

Life on earth is brief.

But legacies live on.

Prayer

God, I celebrate _____ and the life they lived. I give thanks for the time we had and the memories they've left behind. Let their legacy of love be seen in my life. When it is all said and done, let it all point back to love—to you. Amen.

Prompts

Recall a story about someone you lost.
Recall a story about someone who lives.

Practices

Light a candle. Look at the picture of a loved one whom you miss and reflect on the life they lived. What is one thing that you've always admired about them? Their strength? Their work ethic? Their tenacity? Write out your reflections.

Blackout poetry—make a copy of a letter, card, journal entry, text message, post, or recipe left by your loved one. Using a black marker, draw boxes around a selection of words that you can piece together to create a poem or short saying. Completely color over and "black out" the rest of the words that you do not want to use. As you do this, consider how you are creating something new with the legacy of your loved one.

Pieces

I have a box full of words that I did not write,
but one day I will write them all down.
Words you used not just to grow your life,
but to nurture your whole town.

You could have been loud and changed the world
by shouting, "Hey, look at me!"
Instead, you chose to change the world
one by one—so quietly.

The quiet way you led
is still changing hearts today
and words you've written still live and sing
although you've gone away.

I'll do my best to tell your story;
your wisdom will live on.
I only hope they say the same of me
one day when I'm gone.

—Katharine Nadene

The smell of antiquities and homemade patisserie hovers in the air. I'm welcomed in by age-worn arms and hands so thin and fair. Floured jewels and rolling pins, aprons pressed and messed again. Where love is found in gathering, round tables filled and fit for kings. Southern drawls and lemonade. Summer warmth and hymnal sings. When life was slow and time was free, on the creaky green striped swing. We watch the clouds move back and forth. We name them each their own. We tie together flower crowns o'er dripping ice cream cones. And as the night begins to fall we catch lightning in a jar. Those age-worn arms reach high and count the ever-twinkling stars. The whispers and the things we've shared I tuck away and carry. Inside of me for all life's days, and pull out when I am weary. A quiet drifts upon us now, it's time for you to go. You said I was your special girl and that's all I'd need to know. And somewhere between those summer moons and growing up it seems that life moved on without consent and left behind these things. I'm older now and made from you, like clay that's formed and shaped. The glue that bonded childhood dreams and left legacies in wake. You hold my babes, all five of them. You shush them each to sleep. The one you rocked in that small room. And the ones you'd never meet. I see you in my eldest's strength, her strong-willed grit and fire. I hear you in my boy's sweet laugh and find you in his eyes. Our middle girl, you'd love her so, she bears more than your name. With endless words and care for all she's more like you each day. I feel you in the seasons now I see you in my home, where life is lived in-between and love takes root and grows.

—Brittany Smith

15

Let There Be Smallness

Do small things. On repeat.
—Hannah Brencher,
If You Find This Letter

It is the middle of the COVID-19 pandemic. It is summertime, and it is hot and humid. My friend Lauren and I meet at a fountain in the south side of Charlotte. Our boys run together, run their bodies ragged, while the two of us talk about parenting in the pandemic and how we're managing work in our crumbling world.

Freedom Park.

She's lost her job, she tells me. After years of painting faces pretty, after years of doing this one thing for as long as she can remember. A makeup artist. An encourager, telling women they are beautiful, teaching them how to highlight their favorite features, telling them how to learn to really love themselves.

It's the middle of the pandemic, and she's lost her job. Now, she is not sure what she will do.

We talk through the options, every opportunity that came in the emails and phone calls. None of them fit, though. None of them feel right, she says.

I tell her I'll do whatever I can to help. I'll fix up her résumé; I'll look for positions. I want to see her working. But, more than anything, I want to see her happy. When the kids are tired and have had enough of running, we part and go our separate ways.

And it isn't very long until Lauren's Instagram feed is filled with flowers. She says that she's started making floral arrangements and offers them to all kinds of people and places. Then come the flower stems in vases—dahlias, roses, sunflowers, ranunculus.

In time, I realize that I am bearing witness to a private passion turning into a full-blown professional pursuit. As Lauren's business, The Rooted Nest, grows and flourishes, I think back to when it was only just the smallest seed.

Years ago, before the pandemic, Lauren took up making wreaths as a hobby. Not a career, not even a calling. Just a small creative hobby that she cradled on the side.

It was a small thing, and yet it was a significant thing. Because long before making bouquets became a business, it was her humble hobby, one that reflected the simple desire of her heart to bring beauty into the world.

Her small hobby was the start of her awakening a passion.

Her small hobby was the start of awakening a newfound purpose.

There is a fear that you've been holding on to, right there beneath the layers in your heart. You've kept it covered and kept it warm; you've kindled the flames and stoked the fires. You've told yourself that it is not fear at all. You've strained and stressed to dismiss it in every which way.

Still the fear is there, and the fear is real.

It is the fear of smallness, of your being *too* small to be significant. But the impact of small things is not small at all.

It is the proverbial mustard seed giving way to tall trees. It is the five loaves feeding five thousand. It is the widow's mite and the greatness of her gift. It is the babe in Bethlehem—God confounding the big with the small.

It is you and all the smallness that you have to offer. Every act and every bit of art. Indeed, you feel small. Indeed, you may *be* small. Indeed, your days are filled with ordinary smallness.

Small people running wild and rambunctious in your midst. The seemingly small job with small tasks and small pay. The small house with small rooms. The small audience. The small office.

You are a vapor, and you are breath, *yes*.

You are small, but you are not insignificant.

And neither are the things you do and make.

The best essay I ever wrote was the shortest one. It was in my high school English honors class, the one with all the one-hundred-word vocab quizzes I never studied for. My class was given the assignment to write a paper with five paragraphs—an introduction, three body paragraphs, and a conclusion. There was only one catch.

It had to be written on the front of one piece of paper.

Our teacher's reason for the impossibility of this?

That our shortest essay could and would be our strongest. We were challenged to keep our word count small and our main ideas clear. Through this, we learned the careful, courageous act of distilling an idea right down to its very core. We learned how to be cautious and concise with our words. We learned how to include things and when to cut them out. The assignment was hard and impossible. We sighed and struggled through it. But eventually we learned that our teacher was right. The smaller we kept the word count, the stronger our arguments held.

I see a similar opportunity when it comes to social media where we've all been reduced to the character limits of each post. I tend to be lengthy, lyrical, and long-winded (if you haven't noticed by now). I tell whole stories that come full circle. I use repetition, writing the same things over and over. But with social media, I've learned to be brief. I've learned to embrace the art of exactness in expression.

To say what you need and mean what you say.

Nothing more.

Nothing less.

There is something about being introduced to a whole world of a fictional character, about learning their name and hearing their story in the span of just a few minutes.

This is why we love Pixar's short movies. There is a kind of magic in watching the sweetest story unfold in the shortest amount of time. It reminds me of a quote I'd read from Neil Gaiman's MasterClass on storytelling:

> Short stories are tiny windows into other worlds, and other minds, and other dreams. They're journeys you can make to the far side of the universe and still be back in time for dinner.[1]

I remember the magic of a moment like this in my college class on short stories. I had to read "The Moths," a short story written by Helena María Viramontes. I still remember the ending of it closing out with moths, an open window, an *abuela* dying, and a young girl crying, going from grief to relief all in a matter of three pages.

There is one place, in the end, where the girl says:

> There comes a time when the sun is defiant. Just about the time when moods change, inevitable seasons of a day, transitions from one color to another, that hour or minute or second when the sun is finally defeated, finally sinks into the realization that it cannot with all its power to heal or burn, exist forever, there comes an illumination where the sun and earth meet, a final burst of burning red orange fury reminding us that although endings are inevitable, they are necessary for rebirths.[2]

After reading and falling in love with "The Moths," it became clear that this fictional character had gone through a growth. Her resolution came as quick as the cycle of one rising sun. In the smallest gathering of pages, she went from death to life, from young to mature, from not knowing to knowing, from bitter and hurt to healed, seemingly whole.

In the smallest gathering of pages, I, too, grew and healed and matured. For this is the power of short story—its brevity can bring immediate entertainment and relief.

What would it mean for us to see our days like this too? To know that we are only given so much time in a day. To trust that the minutes and moments, as small as they are, truly matter.

Indeed, your days are small, from sunrise to sunset. But they burst and burn with an illumination that makes the most of the cycle of your days and the time offered to you. The smallness of where you are, what you make, and who you are is not only enough—it is *more* than enough.

It is whole in its offering.

It is holy in its offering.

If I will speak on smallness, then I must speak directly to the courage and creativity of small business owners. You might be like me; you might have never believed in the beauty of business. Like me, you might have never dreamed of owning a small business. You might not understand the value of small business. But this has all since changed; I am a believer in businesses—in what they represent and what they do.

It began the week my world collided with COVID-19. Sick on the couch, I couldn't keep up with my whirlwind of deadlines and dreams. Though work and the burden of working on this book pressed on, I had no choice but to stop and rest.

I had no choice but to Netflix.

I had no choice but to relax.

Mia, my dearest friend from college, suggested I watch *Growing Floret*, a four-episode series on the Magnolia Network. She said that my world would be changed, and that I would never be the same. She said I would be blown away, that I would find the rest and hope my soul was so desperately in need of.

I watched *Growing Floret*, only to find that my mind, in fact, had been blown. I was in awe and inspired. I had come to a newfound belief in business.

One by one, I watched the episodes about building gardens, small steps in tackling mountains of debt, failing flower farms, and one woman's dream to change the world in one, small way—through the smallness of flowers.

Floret—even the name itself bears the meaning of smallness.

I sat there, curled up with COVID-19 and on the couch, watching the unfolding story of this business, of this woman Erin Benzakein confessing that, while being a small business owner was nothing she'd ever wanted, she found herself realizing it was better than anything she'd ever imagined.

The story line continued with the elegant and emotional unearthing of her journey and her growing team—their bout with bad crops, disease, flowers dying, and harsh weather. Erin shares how, despite this, her small flower farm was making big impacts.

Then, I hear something in one of the episodes that, once again, blows my mind. A farmer and friend of Erin's speaks into the impact of Floret and other farms. He says, "In the United States, people think that a business is all about money. It's not about money. It's being happy going to work in the morning and waking up excited and ready to go do your thing. A business is about people."[3]

Mia and I go back and forth in conversation, breaking down this concept, right down to the core of it. Processing what this means for our beliefs about business and what it means for our dreams. We ask ourselves where we have been hiding and holding out. Where have we overlooked the impact and the influence of small businesses?

We talk about how we can learn to live in awe of the inherent greatness of small businesses. We talk about what this all means in terms of families, communities, and whole economies.

When it comes to you, I wonder—is there an inkling of a dream or a desire deep inside of you? Is there a small idea or small ideal that lies dormant inside? If so, it might be time to breathe new life into the heart of it; it might be time to curiously consider why it's there and what to do with it.

This isn't about using smallness as a beginning for greatness. This is not about trying to find an American dream somewhere out there waiting for you. It is, however, about speaking into the creative ideas that flood your mind. It is for the ideas you have not been able to put into poems or paintings or words or form or feeling or flesh.

That vision and those values—soaked through and through with innovation and imagination—might be a business. It might be a brand that you envision birthing into the world. It's an art and act that goes beyond mere profit because, at its core, it is really about people.

It might just be a small café, room, or farm that brings together small communities in small ways.

It might just be about the short story of your life—that vapor, that breath—and how you will use it to exhale the heart and hope and hand of God.

Prayer

God, you look with love at that which is small. There is no thing, no person, no place you do not keep your watchful eyes over. Thank you for seeing me; thank you for knowing me. Thank you for speaking deeply to me. Thank you for stirring me to believe the significance of my life, my offerings, and my art. Thank you for using me in the most unassuming ways. Keep me humble; keep my steps small; keep my path sure. Amen.

Prompts

What's hard about being small?

What's holy about being small?

Practices

Read a short story, revel in the beauty of its brevity. Try writing a short story of your own. What lessons do you think you'll learn from this? Do you think it will be easy to write since it will be short, or will it be hard?

Buy seeds, mugs, art, or crafted creations from local businesses and boutiques. Invest in the creativity of your local small businesses; invest in the value they add to your village, town, city, and state.

Pieces

Small leaves, dragged in by wet soles.
A trail leading to wooden church pews,

like petals before a bride.
Autumn pressed into an evergreen carpet.

Isn't this how it always is?
Us, entering Mass with the world on our heels.
Jesus, washing our feet.

—Gina Sares

When the church isn't in church,
Safely contained within four walls,
And we follow His lead beyond
These well-lit and comfortable halls,
Holding high our small but constant light
Within a darkness that tries to maul . . .

What magic would the world then witness?

—Bethany Robin Biter

16

Let There Be Connection

Social media is not new. It has been around for centuries.

—Tom Standage, *Writing on the Wall*

I didn't always use my words for good.

I used to fill pages of journals with soliloquies and secrets, ugly words from deep inside of me, hidden and tucked away, heavy and crumbling.

Ink etched between black lines on blank pages, I'd beat into my brain that I was hopeless and useless. One word at a time, I beat into my brain that everything and everyone around me was hopeless and useless too.

I was a broken, sharp-edged, and bleeding soul, raptured by the curiosities of her mind, led by skepticism and criticism. I was lost in a mental prism and completely unaware of the damage this would cause. Like a cut to the skin, I was etching a chasmic pathway in my brain.

In thinking, creating, releasing, and healing, there is a thin line between purging and poisoning—a thin line between relief and resentment. There is a thin line where, at some point or another, all the brokenness must be remedied, redeemed. This shift took place within me when I traveled to Ecuador on a mission trip with my youth leader, Kevin.

Quito.

"I really think you should go," said Kevin. "I really think this trip could change your life."

"I can't," I told him. *Didn't he know?* This trip to Quito would take place the same week as my beauty pageant.

"I'm already signed up," I said. "I've already started raising money."

"Think about it," he said.

I told him that I would, but I knew that I wouldn't. I didn't care about being on a trip for a week in a country with people who I didn't know, didn't even want to know. I didn't want to be charitable or missional. *I wanted to be famous.* I wanted to be on stage and be known.

Kevin's invitation haunted me. It lingered in my mind every time I thought about the pageant and what I would do with my hair and how I would answer those winning interview questions.

I really think this trip could change your life, his words echoed.

Change my life, and my words, it did.

A long way from home, I sat on grimy bleachers overlooking a dusty soccer field with the skyline of Quito's buildings and the Pichincha stratovolcano in the near horizon. There wasn't enough grass to cover the entire field, so dirt kicked up in my face every time a soccer player came close.

I was there in the middle of Quito's dry season, and I remember being cold, *so cold*, and wrapped up in my favorite hoodie. I was holding a girl whose name I cannot remember but whose face is still carved into my memory.

We sat there, the girl and I, in the chill of the day, watching the kids kick around a black and white *fútbol*. As she nestled against my chest, I rocked her side to side. She had lice in her hair; a lot of the kids did. But I held her, still. Held her because, for the first time in my life, I didn't care about hair.

In that moment, I only cared about my heart, about *her* heart. I only cared to know who she was, how she was, and why this moment mattered. I cared to know where, in all my shattered soul, I would find the space to forever hold the memory of this sweet child.

I wasn't even supposed to be in Quito. I was supposed to be at 1535 Broadway, overlooking Times Square from the New York Marriott Marquis. I was supposed to be getting my hair primped and my gown pressed. I was supposed to be winning that pageant; I was supposed to be taking the crown.

But there I was, looking up into the sky, the cloudless horizon of a blue expanse fenced in by the landscape of Quito's many houses on mountains. There I was watching dogs with three legs run wild. I was not only seeing Quito, but I was seeing a cosmic interconnectedness, a truth breaking through to my broken heart.

It was God's love reaching out to me that day, showing me that we humans are all the same, all desperately in need and in want of love and connection—of being held, heard, and healed.

All of us are desperately in need of being known and needed, found and forgiven, seen and set free.

Not only did that trip change my worldview but it changed my *words*.

After Quito, my writing went from raging about the ruin in the world to wanting to repair it. From despairing about the darkness in the world to desiring to be a part of pushing it back.

I went from picking up the pen for the sake of self-release to using it as a way to usher in world relief. I turned to writing about hope, beauty, truth, and grace, all for the sake of loving and leading others. All for the sake of bringing forth life and light.

It's crazy to me that what God used to mend my broken heart is what he's using to mend the hearts of others. *Hope spilling out into words.* Yet, the most breathtaking part about this is that the same pleasure and purpose is there waiting for *you*.

This is not just *my* story.

This can be *your* story.

There is a book called *Writing on the Wall* by Tom Standage, and it explores social media and how nothing about it is new. Standage writes about social media and the fact that it technically has nothing to do with the technology of phones, computers, and devices but has everything to do with social networking. Social networking and, thus, social media has everything to do with how people desire to connect and dialogue with one another—an ancient concept that isn't in any way modern or novel.

Standage's book took me deep into his research and revelations, leading me to realize that iPads are not the first generation of handheld tools used to record and share information and inspiration. The ancient Romans had also done this with their tablets made of wood and wax.

I learned that before modern social media—long before posting to people's walls on Facebook, long before our claims about social media "getting worse"—the concept of sharing and seeing personal (and profane) opinions in public places already existed. I learned that in ancient Greco-Roman culture, public discourse —as portrayed through *actual* public writings on *actual* physical walls—was commonplace and encouraged. Even expected.[1]

I learned that Rome's beautifully built walls weren't just erected as boundaries of physical space, but as blank pages where everyday people, like you and like me, could write. These etchings of words weren't at all like the modern-day profanity you'd find written on bathroom stalls, but this kind of writing had encouraged, *no*, stoked the flames of public discourse and interactive discussions.

The Smithsonian illustrates this so well in an article about Pompeiian graffiti:

> In the ancient Roman world, graffiti was a respected form of writing—often interactive—not the kind of defacement we now see on rocky cliffs and bathroom stalls. Inside elite dwellings like that of Maius Castricius—a four-story home with panoramic windows overlooking the Bay of Naples that was excavated in the 1960s—she's examined 85 graffito. Some were greetings from friends, carefully incised around the edges of frescoes in the home's finest room. In a stairwell, people took turns quoting popular poems and adding their own clever twists. In other places, the graffiti include drawings: a boat, a peacock, a leaping deer.[2]

I learned that endorsement culture was alive and well, centuries before Twitter, Instagram, and Amazon reviews. In all of this, I learned that what *we* are doing isn't novel, isn't anything new under the sun. Social media—all the writing, the posting, the publicizing, the polarizing, the photographing, the endorsing, the sharing, the resharing, the announcements, the arguments, the self-expression, the self-promotion, *all of it*—has been done before.[3]

It's all been done for the sake of social networking, a way in which people simply connect. And what I really mean to say is that the world isn't really getting any worse, because the opportunity for bad-mouthing someone with words written on walls (physically, and now also virtually) has always been there.

And it *will* always be here.

Social media is not sacrilegious; it is just like any other thing in life, sex, and drink: There is good and there is bad; there is a choice in every chance.

With social media, we are offered a choice, offered the chance to deem it as good or as bad—to call it chaotic because we cannot control it. Or we can use it without abusing it and without abusing others. We can see it as a sacred opportunity and choose to show up to connect and cultivate community.

There will always be darkness and death and destruction at every turn. We already know this about our world; we already know this about life.

We will always stand at the gate of it all—the glare of our screens and the doors of our hearts—with our own demons, our own decay.

It's always been a choice.

It will always be a choice.

It will feel heavy and hard, almost as if we can't possibly bear the task of sifting through the sorrow and systems. You will feel as though you're not sure where to begin, not sure where to fit in.

Not sure how to separate yourself from the noise and riots, the bickering back and forth about who is wrong or right about what.

The good in all of this is that the purpose isn't for your social platforms to be perfect or powerful, for you to be right or to bear yourself to the world without blemish or blame. The point of your writing, posting, sharing, resharing, and discourse—the very reason you sign in to show up—is to etch lines on walls like lines in sand, like Jesus.

Jesus drew lines in the sand before the *scribes* of the law— the only ones allowed, in Jesus's days, to use written words for power or to give pardon.

Jesus, a mere craftsman by trade, unworthy to write away the sins of a sinner, stood there and stooped low—all in a public place where people of power, persuasion, position, political purposes, and platform were *more* than permitted to undermine, diminish, and destroy him.

Nevertheless, he etched lines in sand and wrote away the sins of a sinner (see John 8:1–11).

The truth is that there is space for you to do the same—to stand and sing and speak and sign into public spaces where you can draw lines with words and rewrite truth for a world that is desperate for light.

A world that is in desperate need of grace, and to hear that there is a good God at the ready, able to give all that and more.

———

You are not vain, naive, or corrupt for showing up on social media. You are not offering up yourself; you are offering up the light of the world. Your showing up is not frivolous or fruitless—by way of poems and beauty and preaching and dancing and reels, you are showing and telling the powers that be that darkness has no hold in the presence of the one who has rewritten the laws of grace.

This has always been the heart of God—that every performed, spoken, and written act of love might join in with his work of pushing back the dark. And this counts. *This matters*, not just for the places that you show up for in real life, but for the places you show up in online.

This counts for the connections you make on social media —the Facebook groups, forums, chats, mom meetings, virtual Zoom meetings, Instagram, Slack, Poshmark, and Marketplace —where you are liking and commenting and seeing and reading. You have the choice to make the most out of every chance you get, every chance to ponder the beauty set before you, to name the beautiful and the achingly stunning. To speak with grace where others may speak with words that sting and steal.

Never in a million years would I have imagined that I, the girl who once used her words to do harm within, would one day see a reverse in that curse and use my words to bring hope and help to the world. Never did I ever think I'd sing about beauty, life, or grace.

Never did I think I'd create space for others to connect and cultivate their words to do the same—to push back the darkness in their own lives, to unveil the kind of light that does not burn out.

Yet, here I am, believing that there is space enough to create things that compel others to believe in themselves too. Here I am, believing that there is good in a space that so many believe to be bad. Here I am, telling you to show up, telling you that there is no going around it, there is only going through it.

I thank Pastor Diana for calling me out from the edge of a blue pew, some fifteen years ago. There I was, a teenager, sitting through service and just waiting for someone to tell me that my world wasn't as dark as I believed it to be.

I thank her for using her words to tell me that one day my *own* would soothe more souls than I know. I thank her for telling me that there was space for me out there in the big, wide world. That I was chosen by God to use my words to bring healing and hope. That, so long as I'd continue to choose him, God would make it happen, God would make a way.

Here I am, indebted to my mom who helped put me through college classes where I studied creative writing, where I cultivated a passion for the pursuit of the craft, even when I didn't know how I would use it. Here I am, remembering the day with clarity that I told my mom I'd chosen to study writing.

I remember how she said, without pause or hesitation, that she would be proud of me even if I'd chosen to drive a garbage truck if that's what I'd really wanted.

Here I am today, still forging words to be seen by other human hearts, still telling myself to believe that all of this really is like drawing lines in the sand. And, *goodness*, how the same is dangerously true for you.

How the world may or may not—like Jesus's mysterious words in the sand—ever know or see all the words *you* write or things *you* make. Nevertheless, a life can still be changed. A life, *your life*, can still be saved. All because you wrote, spoke, made, or created something. All because you dared to push back the dark.

In terms of eternity, your creativity really does matter. There is a purpose that far outweighs your platform and a cosmic cause for the way we all connect in the ways we do. It's about joining God in his restorative work.

It's about seeing his heart.

It's about being his hand.

Prayer

God, I want eyes that see beyond all that is bad. Give me sight to see the good. Cultivate a compassion within me for those I don't know. I give thanks for the gift of social media. I give thanks for the way you made our hearts crave connection. Help me find my way in this digital world. Use me to help others who are finding their way too. Amen.

Prompts

What do you like about social media?
What are you learning from social media?

Practices

Follow someone on social media whose views, perspective, opinions, beliefs, and published pieces oppose that of your own. Learn from them and learn to love them. Beyond centering discussions to dissuade, engage with this person's posts with the sole purpose of deepening your capacity to connect and care.

Plan a frequently recurring time to step away from social media. Make this time an intentional break filled with respite and rest. Partake in activities that will soothe your senses. Pray for the people you show up to serve.

Pieces

I once believed I had to wrap up every post with a positive, overt Christian message. Now I find goodness in the abstract, the subjective, in the kind of writing that may lead to more questions instead of absolute certainty. The more I write, the more I find my way, the more I share, the more I learn from so many of you. There is goodness in the wrestle, in the seeking, in the embrace of the unknown and the wonder of it all.

—Sarah Southern

If I could I would wrap up words in a beautiful box and send them your way. I would tell you that all the little things you do in a day are important. You are never "just" a _____ . I would remind you that perfection is an illusion and you no longer need to carry that burden or chase that standard. I would tell you, as I tell myself, that productivity does not determine your worth. I would encourage you to stir up those long-lost passions and go for it—make the art, sing the songs, write the book, learn to dive, create that community. Allow yourself to dream and become more fully alive in the pursuit of them. I would remind you that you are fabulous! There is no one quite like you in all the world. Your wrinkles, insecurities, extra pounds, anxieties, or weaknesses do not disqualify you from bringing your special gift to humanity. You are needed, just as you are. I guess these little squares will have to fill in for tiny wrapped boxes coming in the mail.

—Sue Fulmore

Let There Be Laughter

Comedy is medicine. Not coloured sweeties to rot the teeth with.

—Trevor Griffiths, *Comedians*

I have a friend named Ryan Rich. Sometimes I call him Rich by accident. It's really a mistake on my part, but it's no matter to him. He's the kind of guy who finds things like that funny. *Facebook.*

On March 19, 2019, Ryan wrote on his Facebook wall to announce that he'd discovered he had a brain tumor:

> A couple weeks ago we found out that I have a benign brain tumor, a little smaller than a golf ball, called an acoustic neuroma. I had gone to the doctor about some sudden hearing loss in my right ear, and an MRI revealed that the cause was a tumor growing over the hearing nerve and pushing into my brain stem. I am planning to have surgery in a few weeks which, along with removing the tumor, will take what remains of the

hearing on my right side and require a significant recovery. My medical team has recommended that I spend some time on a beach after surgery to keep myself from the kind of overexertion that could lead to setbacks, and I am going to work hard to be a compliant patient in that regard . . .

Because it's arguably weird to talk to someone who just found out they have a brain tumor (in this scenario, me), here are some thoughts:

1. I'm not particularly happy about having a brain tumor, but lots of us go through hard and scary things—and many of you (my friends) have gone through much worse. For the most part I am amazingly grateful for what I have and am hopeful for my recovery. Let's please not be too sad about this.

2. I'm fine with jokes. That's my thing. I realize brain tumors aren't inherently funny . . .

From my experience on the other side of things like this, I know some of you will want to do *something* but not know what to do. Because my surgery isn't for a few weeks, we really don't need anything specific right now. But because I have your attention (and, ahem, a brain tumor . . .), here's an idea.

Benign Pranks!!

I love pranking and surprising my friends, and I would love to see that spirit unleashed while I'm getting ready for and recovering from surgery. So if you're up for it, consider pulling some benign (i.e., gentle, kind, no glitter, etc.) pranks on the people in your circles.

Lots of love and happy pranking.

In all my years of living and loving others, never have I met a soul who wanted to unleash pranks in the middle of crisis. Never have I met someone who politely declined being added to prayer lists, who intentionally asked to not be told "I'm so sorry."

I am not saying that those who ask for, need, or want these things are wrong or weak. I am saying, however, that there is something uniquely powerful about Ryan's request for pranks. He wasn't hiding behind a need to deflect the reality of his situation. He wasn't running away from the family who loved him or the friends who cared for him. He knew very well what he was asking for and, quite frankly, what it was that he needed and wanted.

Joy.

He wanted to be surrounded and surprised by joy, wanted to receive it but also wanted to reflect and release it. And it is a beautiful thing, this joy. An understated strength and faith. Joy is a way of looking into *and* reflecting love. It is seeing the good, and it's being the good.

I share Ryan's post from Facebook because the very thing I hoped that Ryan would experience is the very thing I've found I've experienced myself. His story, his experience, has been formative in the cultivation of my own joy.

In the weeks and months and years ahead, as I'd come to navigate the aftershocks of a global pandemic and the need to make difficult decisions, I realized I had a choice and say in the matter. I had a choice in how I'd express my reactions, as well as what I would permit from others in terms of *their* reactions.

In the weeks and months ahead, and when it came time to walk out my own health journey—in those hours before my biopsy, underneath the spinning CAT scan—I realized *I* had a choice. I had the choice to call for and cultivate joy.

Once I caught a fraction of an ad on YouTube for a MasterClass on comedy by Steve Martin. In the first few seconds of his face flashing across my screen, I heard him say, "I am always thinking of the joke."

Intrigued, I let the ad play to see what else he would say. I watched him improvising, acting, miming, teaching other comedians, and laughing.

"You are a thought machine," he said. "Everything you see and experience is usable."[1]

The ad reminded me of the "Went with the Wind!" comedy sketch from the tenth season of *The Carol Burnett Show*. Carol Burnett plays Starlet O'Hara as a parody and, with the help of her team, she creates a costume that involves Carol ripping a pair of curtains off a window and dressing up in them.

She walks down the stairs and tells the man who says that her dress is beautiful that she "saw it in a window and just *had* to have it."[2]

Maybe you know that sketch, or maybe you don't. Either way, it's such a classic example of someone, as Steve Martin says, using anything and everything just to make a joke. It's such a classic example of how comedy works and *why* it works. It's the paradoxical expectations, the presentation of something *other* than what we would expect. It embodies exaggeration and allows absurdity.

A *curtain for a dress.*

Pranks for a tumor.

These paradoxes essentially provide a reprieve from the repeats of life, the day in and day out of the mundane, of what is predictable, memorized, and etched into our brains. Comedy brings the break our hearts and minds desperately need and hope for.

How good is God that he would make for us a way of rising above what is hard and heavy in life? What a gift that, in the midst of wounds, wars, pain, and pandemics, comedy could come—could surprise the way we see and unburden the way we breathe.

The power in the work of Charlie Chaplin, of silent acting, is that it pervades language and culture. Beyond saying, it takes *seeing*. This is the creativity of our God, too, that there would be this one, beautiful way of connecting people across cultures, across languages, across continents, and across countries. That every human might hear humor the same. Might recognize it—in a smile or a smirk—and relate to it and therefore find reprieve *through* it.

I took an acting class in high school, and I will never forget walking into the classroom and seeing a circle of chairs. Our teacher asked us to pick a chair and to sit in the circle. He told us we'd be learning to laugh by looking at each other and simply resolving to do so.

At first, there was only an awkward silence and eyes darting at unsure faces.

What were we supposed to laugh at?

Who were we supposed to laugh at?

Then, there was a snort, and soon the whole circle filled and roared with laughter. None of us could keep from laughing or name who started it. To this day, I can't recall the names of the ones who sat beside me in that class.

But I remember the prompt to laugh and the feeling of the impossibility of it. I remember how fast composure gave way to comedy in a circle of gathered students, all different, but really all the same. Deep down, each one of us possessed the ability to laugh at and be amused by the absurdity of our situation.

Sit in a circle for class.

Laugh on purpose.

This moment in my life taught me that, too often, we take the creativity of comedy for granted. We forget that humor is unconventionally healing. We forget that laughter unwittingly restores us to peace within ourselves, even peace within the world.

Our human brains can become so fixated on the things we know and understand. Sometimes, we need to see things that exceed our expectations, things that entertain our astonishment.

The invitation, then, is that we can choose to be amazed, choose to be surprised. We can position ourselves to be in places and with people who will undo the constructs of our thinking, the rituals and routines that we've come to accept. I read in an article that

> Great comedy clarifies reality in some way. It changes our perceptions rather than simply confirming them. Humans are meaning-making animals; we make sense of our lives by building up a delicate, unnoticed edifice of symbolic rituals and routines around us. By making surprising but plausible connections between seemingly disconnected things, comedy makes this edifice of shared, unspoken meanings visible. And, best of all, it can do this in an instant, without having to over-explain itself, or indeed be self-consciously "edgy." Comedy can say, with an elegant economy, what everyone knows but no one had noticed before—which is why a good joke isn't just a cheap laugh at someone else's expense; it is a thing of beauty.[3]

This is why we love the late night shows; this is why we love comedy tours. This is why videos go viral and challenges trend on TikTok. This is how and why memes matter. It is not because they make *fun* of, rather they make *sense* of. Memes are medicine for our brains which can't help but be in a constant search for connection. Comedy, all clever and creative, comes in and gives way for these connections to be made. It is healing and liberating and humbling and whole—your impulse to laugh and crave what is comical.

And you do not only have to clap at comedy; you can *create* it. You can stand on stages and lead crowds to laughter. You can go to your screen and create reels with hilarity and humor.

You can bring your personality; you can be your funny self. You can be the one who gives the punch lines, pulls the pranks, and reveals the magic tricks. You can bring that element of exaggeration, which not only elicits laughter but positions people to be *surprised*.

The breathtaking thing about this is that God can and *is* doing the same. God is always in the business of positioning people to be *surprised*. He is always, as my childhood pastor Kenneth Tinch used to say, making us amazingly aware.

God invites us to see the world the way that he does, but he also maintains a loving boundary to remind us that his thoughts are not our thoughts, and his ways are not our ways. In this, he is always inviting us to stand *amazingly aware* and in awe of the work of his hands.

He is dazzling us now.

He has dazzled us before.

He will dazzle us forever.

Prayer

God, dazzle me with your delight and surprise me with your joy. I want to see you in a new light. I want to know your heart and share it too. Tickle my soul to overflow with the expression of your wonder. Humor me with the paradox of your hope in our world. Open my eyes to be amazed by your great love. Amen.

Prompts

Retell (or reenact) a scene from a play
or movie that makes you laugh.

Retell (or reenact) a memory from your life
that makes you laugh.

Practices

Learn about the life of a comedian. Study their story and dive deep into their craft and comedy, beliefs about humor, work, art, and life. Look at whether they navigated any hardships or traumas. What can you learn from their life? How does this help you appreciate the art they offer(ed) to the world?

Play a prank on a friend or family member. Keep it clean, practice good (appropriate) timing, and, at all possible costs, avoid using glitter.

Pieces

Joy: A wistful grin upon a face of someone who's finished a hard day's work.

—Lamar Gibbs

She springs up like the dandelions in spring,
and, if you're not careful,
you may mistake her for ordinary.

She nourishes your soul in times of deepest despair,
shields you from becoming too hard, too stagnant,
too forlorn,
brings you back to a place of peace in your body, your
soul, your mind,
offers you a moment to lay down your burdens and
bask in goodness,
soothes the tender places of your spirit aching to be
gathered up, to be seen, to be held.

She is the smile on your child's face,
the warm mug that touches your lips,
the laughter shared among friends,
the leaves tickling your face as they fall,
the moon lighting the way, and
the sun drenching your face in radiance.

And, maybe (just maybe)
it's time we remember:
Joy, too, comes in the mourning.

—Katie Drobina

18

Let There Be Light

Had I words I could tell of origin, of God's hands bloody with
birth at first light . . . I could tell of the splintered sun. I could
articulate the night sky, had I words.

—N. Scott Momaday, "Prayer for Words"

I stood in the parking lot, just outside of my college dorm
room, and I told myself that I was going to become a pho-
tojournalist. I told myself that I was going to spend my life
traveling, taking photos, and writing about every little happening, both in the world and within my own.

But this was before Instagram was invented, before everyone
became photojournalists with iPhones.

Christie Hall.

Walking back from class, I'd thought about how I always
loved photography, how I'd always found photographs of family
and friends utterly captivating. I kept a portrait of my cousin
Chenna in my journal around the time that she died of leuke-

216

mia. I'd only met her a handful of times, but she was so beautiful and kind that the thought of holding on to her photo felt like keeping her alive in my memory.

When I found out that Nyack College would be offering a photography class, I signed up right away. I bought my camera using a school loan, trusting that the investment would be well worth it. It was a night class, which took away the nerves I'd felt about it. It felt like a guilty pleasure to be able to take a class on creativity in the middle of my essays and exams. It gave my mind the space it needed so that I could fully immerse myself in something different, something new.

In the class, I was introduced to a whole new world of dimensions, rules, and creative concepts. Rules that serve as guidelines resulting in skills to capture and create beautiful images. Rules like the rule of thirds, frames within frames, and negative space.

But there is one thing, one thought that deeply captivated me.

It is the camera's aperture, the opening in the camera that lets light in or keeps light out. To this day, I am still learning how to master and control aperture. Nevertheless, I believe that this concept, this setting of control, offers truth for the way we can and should live our lives.

A camera's aperture, or rather a photographer's ability to work with and adjust the aperture, means everything for the kind and quality of photos being taken.

The greater the aperture, the more light that comes in. The more light, the brighter the photo. The smaller the aperture, the less light that comes in. The less light, the darker the photo.

I almost do not have to explain the implications of this; this concept of control nearly speaks for itself. It speaks for the control that we, too, possess in our art and lives.

The more light we let in, the brighter our lives.
The more dark we let out, or push back, the brighter the world.

I started this book with the creation story, and that is how I'll end this book. I will return to those same words and go back to the story of God before the garden, back to when there is only a vastness and void—a world without shape or shadow or light.

I will return to this story and retell it the best way I know how—*in poem*:

> Eternity echoes
> before Eden.
>
> Divinity dances with darkness,
> commands and calls
> light to *come*
> and *to be*.
>
> With light, he creates. But,
> with light, he *controls*.
>
> Orders chaos.
> Orders cosmos.
>
> With his being.
> With his breath.
>
> Burns darkness
> with boundary.
>
> Makes goodness
> our right.
>
> *Hallelujah*,
> light has come.

Though darkness
lingers,

Son lives
on.

The creation story is about more than just creativity. It is about God's power and goodness and justice on display. Light is not just bright; it is a boundary. It is a push against the dark. And we are invited into this work by way of being and breathing.

When we practice creativity—when we participate in it and partake of it—it is like we are controlling the aperture of a camera, opening the hole wider and working with God to push back the darkness.

You may feel broken, imperfect. You may wonder whether you are inventive enough. You may wonder whether the words you write—or the meals you make, or the portraits you paint, or the sketches you animate, or the rooms you design, or the sermons you speak, or the casting calls you get called to—are of any weight. You may wonder if any of it is worth it.

But you have seen the light, and you can *be* the light.

By way of creating, you are bringing forth light.

By way of making, you are making God known.

I'll tell you about a young girl who was a lamb in the Christmas plays every year. My brothers and I were the sheep and the cows, whatever four-legged creatures that could blend clamorous children into a harmonious choir, singing songs about Jesus, telling the world how he came to save us at Christmastime, all the lambs and the sheep and the cows.

And when we weren't dressed like little lambs and little sheep at Christmas, we were dressed like Christmas in New York every Sunday of the year, all bundled up in lengths and layers.

My mom and dad told me the stories of the church we grew up in, and how we were all taught to keep covered, taught that women could only wear dresses and skirts, taught that it was wrong to go to the movies, or to go ice-skating, or to wear jewelry.

As a young girl growing up in church, I had somehow come to think that anything relating to or revolving around Jesus always came back to being good or being bad. I had come to think that doing the right thing meant just plain doing what you were told—like wearing dresses and cleaning up your room, like good little lambs caroling about Jesus at Christmastime.

I had come to think that God was just a story to learn. He was a song to memorize in children's church and vacation Bible school, just another character from a book—like The Mad Hatter from *Alice in Wonderland*[1] or Wilbur in *Charlotte's Web*[2]—that I'd learned about and learned from, but had never been loved by.

The hardest part about this story is that I know it is not uniquely my own. I know there are others, maybe even you, who cradle moments and memories that have tangled you into questioning whether Jesus, God's own Son, is anything more than a story from a book.

In so many ways, Jesus has been whittled down to the smallest wooden figurine in a nativity scene. *So sweet, so precious, so gracious* we think him to be.

Which is true, but it's not the whole truth. Because Jesus is also wild and untamed. He is fierce, an all-consuming fire, the bright-burning light of the world.

He is not merely a kind man who once lived. *He is kingdom.*
He is not merely a good character in a story. *He is God.*

I can't help but be fascinated by the creativity of Jesus who, an ordinary craftsman, cultivated a craft and a skill that consisted of both creating *and* fixing things. When you think about it, it's kind of cosmically ironic. The fact that Jesus went from working with his hands—both creating *and* repairing with them—to stepping into a ministry that consisted of nearly the same.

Jesus created—water to wine, food to feed thousands, community.

Jesus also repaired—calmed raging seas, healed the sick, brought death to life.

The act of creating does more than create things; it *restores* things. It *calms* things. It *heals* things. It *saves* things. It lets light into our lives, and it pushes back darkness.

This Jesus, this light of the world, cannot be taken lightly. And neither can our call to be like him. In a sermon entitled "The Mind of Christ," my friend and pastor Kate Haynes Murphy preached this:

> The kinds of stories that Jesus tells have a special name because they're different from the kinds of stories we tell. The stories Jesus tells are alive, they are unruly. They do not soothe, affirm, reassure, or settle us. They do not answer questions, they raise them. They do not resolve tension, they create tension. They disturb us. As they are intended to do. The stories Jesus tells are called parables and they're holy because they give us a window into the dangerously holy mind of Christ.

The mind of Christ is bent on his father's business. It is bent on bringing the dawn of a new day to this world that, for now, tilts dark, damned, and broken.

And though the work is heavy, the work is also holy.

There may be more questions than answers. More mysteries than miracles. More worries than wonders. More hurt than hope. But the light has come, and it *is* holding back the dark.

This world, right here, spinning right before your eyes, burns with brokenness and heaves with hurt. There are human hearts right here, right before your hope-filled hands.

These humans are the people who have been placed before you—they are your children, your neighbors, your students, your doctors, your virtual clients, your strangers in passing. And they are waiting for someone to tell them a story—or for someone to build them a table, or paint them a painting, or sing them a song, or write them a book, or knit them a blanket, or open the door of a hospitable home. They are waiting for someone to tell them *hold on.*

And, my God, what purpose, that by creating, we can bring forth light.

What pleasure, that by making, we can make him known.

Both in the world and in our own.

There are two thoughts about light and life that remain. Two final things that I want to whisper to you as you near the last exhale of this book.

In photography, there is both deep depth of field and shallow depth of field. Neither of them is more important than the other as both of these result in breathtaking photographs.

The difference is in their function.

Shallow depth of field speaks of photos that have one specific area of focus. Deep depth of field speaks of photos that keep everything in the photo clear and in focus.

You see this all the time—through headshots, photos in magazines, on Instagram, and even in the family photos you take each year. We love photos with shallow depth of field because they focus on what matters most in the photo. *Your face. Their hands. The dew on flower petals.* In photos with shallow depth of field the background is blurred and focus on one specific area is clear.

With great depth of field, everything matters; everything is in focus and everything is clear. This is your landscape photography —the photos that beg for *whole* subjects and settings to be captured.

I could tell you about settings and f-stops and modes. I could tell you more about aperture, lighting, and rules of photography.

But we don't need to know everything in order to know this one thing.

God also creates with both shallow and deep depth of field in mind.

We see this when he declares: *Let there be light* (Gen. 1:3). This was God creating *light*, but it was also God declaring Christ. Creator God didn't just hang the sun, moon, and stars to push back the darkness in that one specific moment. He was declaring that all darkness, for all time to come, will not stand against the light of the world, the light of his Son.

In the beginning, God did more than create—he did more than make animals, man, and a world with life. He was demonstrating pleasure, and he was demonstrating purpose. God was demonstrating his heart, as well as the power in his hand to cradle a world that involved his care.

He was pushing back the darkness, both for the moment and for eternity. He was pushing back the darkness for the world, and for you and me.

In the creation story, we see a God—both deeply intimate and widely concerned—serving the present and the future all at the same time. As we create, we offer up the same. Our smallest acts of art serve us in the moment and save us for the future.

We are presently creating for the sake of our pleasure.

But we are also a part of a bigger purpose to reflect God's heart for the world. Beyond creating for ourselves, we are joining God in *his* creation, in *his* proclamation of Jesus, the light of the world.

The one who pushes back the darkness and will forevermore. Amen.

Prayer

God, thank you for the light. Thank you for your light in the world and your light in me. May the light of your love shine from my spirit and through my skin. Use the words on my lips and the work of my hands. To the ends of the earth with you. To the ends of the earth for you. Amen.

Practices

Wake up early to watch the sunrise. Stay up late to watch the sunset. Marvel at the sun, the stars, and the moon. Ponder creation, both God's act (process) of it and the art (product) of it.

Practice photography. Use your phone to take photos of objects with and in light. The sun, stars, moon, mirrors, glass, candles, decorative lights. Contemplate the impact of light (or lack thereof) as you take pictures. If you have a camera with advanced features, consider the impact of adjustments made to the aperture. Record your ruminations and observations. Further your skills by learning to work the settings available to you.

Prompts

Where and when do you see darkness in the world?
Where and when do you see light in the world?

Pieces

It happened one morning, that dawn light crept over the ridge beyond, gold reaching the new buds and the tiny leaves of our trees, turning them to confetti—a million shimmering specks thrown up high by invisible hands and caught mid-air, as in a polaroid.

—Abbie Herring

May you stay open to the evidence of Hope now, searching for and finding unexpected glimmers among the shadows.

—Kristin Vanderlip

Acknowledgments

Shin, our family is my favorite work of art. Creating a life with you is my greatest dream come true. You are loving, patient, forgiving, and kind, and my life is deeply rich because of you. Thank you for loving me, knowing me, teaching me, sacrificing for me, and inspiring me. Cheers to more years of making things together. Yours in Limbo, forever.

Milo and Aaro, words will never express the way my heart bursts with joy at the witness of your wonder, play, imagination, laughter, and brilliance. You teach me every day to keep from living with my eyes shut. Writing this book while raising you has been the hardest but holiest gift to unravel. Thank you for the front-row seat to all your living and loving.

Mom and Dad, behind the poems and pieces that I write are your lessons, revelations, stories, memories, passions, and professional pursuits. Mom, not once have you ever withheld your support in my travels, wild ideas, and passions. Your belief in me gave me the space and faith to become. Dad, your lessons and lectures took root in me deeper than you will ever know. I love you both and will always honor you.

Jordan, Ben, and Zack, our childhood memories return to me on the days I need them most, the days when I need and want to be reminded of the depth and delight that come from the simple pleasures of building forts with blankets, riding bikes in driveways, and catching crayfish in creeks. Each of you are artists in your own right. Your sketches, movie scripts, acting, modeling, musicality, intellect, reasoning, and laughter will always bring a smile to my face. Always proud of who each of you are.

Grandma, from our conversations on books and movies, to your hospitality and home-cooked meals, to the way you love—I see glimpses of you in the little things that I do, and it is the sweetest gift to be reminded of how much you've impacted my life. I hope it brings you deep, sustainable joy knowing you've cultivated creativity in all our lives. From tinsel on trees to hand-sewn dresses—we will remember it all. I love you. *Shmily.*

To my many aunts, uncles, and cousins, it brings me deep pride knowing we are tethered together. I honor the story of our families and hope that beauty, passion, and rest will always be yours to see and to share.

Kevin, Alli, Renee, the words in my head and heart became a book because of each of you. Kevin, you mentored me in my writing and believed in me long before anyone else did. Behind the scenes, you fostered the good and dared to challenge all that needed growth. Know that your faithful guidance in my life is precisely why this book became. Alli and Renee, you saw something in me that was ready to emerge from secrecy to be shared with the world. Thank you for calling me out, holding my hand, having my back, and speaking life into my dreams. I will forever be in awe of the way you both make way for the writers and creatives coming behind you.

To Faith Assembly of God, Crosspointe, The Grove Church, and Journey Church, thank you for your endless love, support, patience, and prayers in my living, loving, growing, failing, falling, serving, and writing. John and Kivian, I am who and how I am because you unreservedly loved and led the little girl I was. Thank you for holding space for me in your home, hearts, and in the arts. Susan, I have journals upon journals filled with words spoken by both you and Ken. Kate, words cannot express the depth and breadth of your inspiration and ministry to me, and your friendship *with* me. Matt, I am thankful for your generous heart which made way and space for Shin to be present in countless ways throughout this process.

To the friends who have held me, known me, and walked through the deepest hurts and hopes with me. Mia, you are my sister and I love you. Rebecca, Meredith, KJ, Morgan, Katie, Sarah, Tiffany, Jazmine, Harry, Lamar, Joanne, Angel, Kayla, Courtney, and Lauren. I love and believe in each of you so deeply. Thank you for seeing my heart and the gift of growing in fellowship with you.

To my Proverbs 31 Ministries and (in)courage sisters, you lead with grace and light and remind me that our words have weight in this world. It is a dream come true and an honor to stand alongside each of you. Forever in awe of the way our separate stories join together to lift up the one and true story. Thank you for holding space for me, embracing me, and loving me.

To Andrea and my team at Revell Books, thank you for believing in me and creating *with* me. To my editor, Kelsey, who not only saw beauty in my words, but saw art that belonged and books to become—you are making this world shine better and brighter, one story at a time. You are not just publishing books, you're pushing back darkness from the narrative of this broken world. Your work is art, and so are you, friend.

To BraveWorks, Called Creatives, and Entrusted Women, thank you for welcoming me into your communities that cultivate compassion and creativity. I am forever thankful for the students, staff, and professors of Nyack College who indelibly touched my life, called me deeper, and gave wings to my creativity.

Thank you to Hans Zimmer and the late Jóhann Jóhannsson; your music was the soundtrack of every writing and editing session. Thank you for your art and the true stories that you tell with mere musicality.

Main Street Coffee & Coworking in Huntersville, Good Drip Coffee in Davidson, Lake Norman State Park, and the parking lot of Goodwill, thank you for giving me safe places to wander and write in the middle of a pandemic.

To the beautiful humans of Fallow Ink, your honest words and works of art move the deepest part of me. When the world is dark and grim and broken and hopeless, it is and will always be your words that come breaking and beaming through. I believe in you, and I hope this book will always remind you to believe in you too.

To you, reader, for bending your heart to hear these words, for trusting that there is truth to be found on these thin, wispy pages, and for the beauty and light that will burst forth into the world because of all the ways you'll let art be in and through you.

Notes

Invitation: May Your Light Break Forth

1. Mihaly Csikszentmihalyi, *Creativity: Flow and the Psychology of Discovery and Invention* (New York: HarperCollins, 1996), 199.

Chapter 1 Let There Be Bareness

1. Ann Voskamp, *The Broken Way: A Daring Path into the Abundant Life* (Grand Rapids: Zondervan, 2016), 12.

2. Jeffery M. Leonard, *Creation Rediscovered: Finding New Meaning in an Ancient Story* (Peabody, MA: Hendrickson, 2020), 164–65.

3. Leonard, *Creation Rediscovered*, 165.

4. Madeleine L'Engle, *Walking on Water: Reflections on Faith and Art* (New York: Convergent, 2016), 4.

5. Lore Wilbert Ferguson, "The Blackbird Letters #6: Writing as Protest," Sayable, June 10, 2021, https://www.sayable.net/blog/2021/6/10/the-blackbird -letters-6-writing-as-protest.

Chapter 2 Let There Be Goodness

1. José Andrés, "José Andrés: The Power of Food," *National Geographic*, April 15, 2014, https://www.nationalgeographic.com/culture/article/chef-jose -andres-why-food-is-important-to-me?loggedin=true.

2. Aarti Sequeira, "How Cooking is Holy Ground to Experience God," (in)courage, September 25, 2021, https://www.incourage.me/2021/09/how -cooking-is-holy-ground-to-experience-god.html.

Chapter 3 Let There Be Likeness

1. E. H. Gombrich, *Art and Illusion: A Study in the Psychology of Pictorial Representation*, vol. 5 of *The A.W. Mellon Lectures in the Fine Arts* (Princeton: Princeton University Press, 1956), 182–202.

2. L'Engle, *Walking on Water*, 33.

3. Artists Network Staff, "Drawing Basics: How to Capture a Likeness When You Draw People," Artists Network, April 14, 2009, https://www.artistsnetwork.com/art-mediums/drawing/drawing-basics-how-to-capture-a-likeness-when-you-draw-people/.

4. Rachel Marie Kang, "Black Books Matter," *Christianity Today*, July 24, 2020, https://www.christianitytoday.com/ct/2020/july-web-only/black-books-matter.html.

Chapter 4 Let There Be Courage

1. K.J. Ramsey, *This Too Shall Last: Finding Grace When Suffering Lingers* (Grand Rapids: Zondervan, 2019), 31.

2. James Hall, *The Self-Portrait: A Cultural History* (London: Thames & Hudson, 2014), 8.

3. Hall, *The Self-Portrait*, 9.

4. Hall, *The Self-Portrait*, 31–49.

5. Frida Kahlo, "The Broken Column," Google Arts & Culture, accessed March 8, 2022, https://artsandculture.google.com/asset/the-broken-column-frida-kahlo/EgGMbMFBQrAe3Q?hl=en.

6. Frida Kahlo, "Frida Kahlo Quotes," FridaKahlo.org, accessed March 8, 2022, https://www.fridakahlo.org/frida-kahlo-quotes.jsp.

7. Anna Abraham, *The Neuroscience of Creativity* (Cambridge, UK: Cambridge University Press, 2018), 121.

8. *Inception*, directed by Christopher Nolan (Burbank, CA: Warner Home Video, 2010), DVD.

Chapter 5 Let There Be Home

1. Mary Oliver, "Sleeping in the Forest," Poet Seers, accessed March 8, 2022, https://www.poetseers.org/contemporary-poets/mary-oliver/mary-oliver-poems/sleeping-in-the-forest/.

2. Joy Harjo, "My House is the Red Earth," Poetry Foundation, accessed March 26, 2022, https://www.poetryfoundation.org/poems/51640/my-house-is-the-red-earth.

Chapter 6 Let There Be Play

1. "Hans Zimmer Performs Inception 'Time' – The World of Hans Zimmer," YouTube video, 4:50, posted by "Film Music Fan," November 23, 2018, https://youtu.be/xdYYN-4ttDg.

2. "Writing to Picture with Hans Zimmer," YouTube video, 9:11, posted by "Mix with The Masters," July 17, 2020, https://youtu.be/sj2PdzPzyYY.

3. Courtney Ellis, *Happy Now: Let Playfulness Lift Your Load and Renew Your Spirit* (Carol Stream, IL: Tyndale, 2021), 20–21.

4. C. S. Lewis, *The Lion, the Witch and the Wardrobe* (London: Geoffrey Bles, 1950).

5. *Tolkien*, directed by Dome Karukoski (Los Angeles, CA: Fox Searchlight Pictures, 2019).

6. Jon Miltimore, "J.R.R. Tolkien's Destitute Mom Gave Him One Hell of an Education," Intellectual Takeout, August 31, 2017, https://www.in tellectualtakeout.org/article/jrr-tolkiens-destitute-mom-gave-him-one-hell -education/.

Chapter 7 Let There Be Fairy Tales

1. *Transformers*, directed by Michael Bay (Glendale, CA: Dreamworks, 2007), DVD, 2:02:20.

2. L'Engle, *Walking on Water*, 46.

3. *The Wizard of Oz*, directed by Victor Fleming (Beverly Hills, CA: Metro-Goldwyn-Mayer, 1939).

4. *Beauty and the Beast*, directed by Gary Trousdale and Kirk Wise (Burbank, CA: Walt Disney Feature Animation, 1991).

5. Chris Claremont, "Origin of Storm," *Uncanny X-Men (1963)* #102, (New York: Marvel Comics, 1976); Chris Claremont, "Juggernaut Appearance," *Uncanny X-Men (1963)* #103, (New York: Marvel Comics, 1977).

6. *The Walking Dead*, created by Frank Darabont (New York: AMC, 2010–2022).

7. *Jingle Jangle: A Christmas Journey*, directed by David E. Talbert (Nashville, TN: Golden Girl, 2020), Netflix.

8. *Harry Potter and the Deathly Hallows: Part 2*, directed by David Yates (Burbank, CA: Warner Bros. Pictures; London: Heyday Films; London: Moving Picture Company, 2011), DVD, 1:06:47.

9. *Toy Story*, directed by John Lasseter (Burbank, CA: Walt Disney Pictures; Emeryville, CA: Pixar Animation Studios, 1995).

10. *The Chronicles of Narnia: The Lion, the Witch and the Wardrobe*, directed by Andrew Adamson (Burbank, CA: Walt Disney Pictures; Los Angeles: Walden Media, 2005).

11. *Sister Act*, directed by Emile Ardolino (Burbank, CA: Touchstone Pictures, 1992).

12. George Eilot, *Silas Marner* (London, UK: Penguin Books, 2003).

13. *The Lord of the Rings: The Return of the King*, directed by Peter Jackson (Burbank, CA: New Line Cinema; Wellington, New Zealand: WingNut Films, 2003).

14. *Anne of Green Gables*, directed by Kevin Sullivan (Toronto: Sullivan Entertainment, 1985).

15. *Little Women*, directed by Gillian Armstrong (Culver City, CA: Columbia Pictures; Culver City, CA: DiNovi Pictures, 1994).

16. *Black Panther*, directed by Ryan Coogler (Burbank, CA: Marvel Studios; Burbank, CA: Walt Disney Pictures, 2018).

17. *The Lord of the Rings: The Fellowship of the Ring*, directed by Peter Jackson (Burbank, CA: New Line Cinema; Wellington, New Zealand: Wing-Nut Films, 2001).

18. *Harry Potter and the Deathly Hallows: Part 2*; J. K. Rowling, *Harry Potter and the Deathly Hallows* (New York: Arthur A. Levine Books, 2009).

19. Lawrence Yuen, "On the Harry Potter Debate: A Catholic Perspective Today," The Myth Pilgrim, February 10, 2021, https://themythpilgrim.com/2021/02/10/harrypotter/.

20. David C. Downing, "Sub-Creation or Smuggled Theology: Tolkien contra Lewis on Christian Fantasy," C. S. Lewis Institute, accessed March 8, 2022, https://www.cslewisinstitute.org/node/1207.

21. Mike Snider, "Two-thirds of Americans, 227 Million, Play Video Games. For Many Games Were An Escape, Stress Relief in Pandemic," *USA Today*, July 13, 2021, https://www.usatoday.com/story/tech/gaming/2021/07/13/video-games-2021-covid-19-pandemic/7938713002/.

22. *The Legend of Zelda: The Ocarina of Time*, Nintendo 64 (United States: Nintendo, 1998).

23. Will Harris, "The Best Story-Driven Video Games," The Gamer, October 29, 2021, https://www.thegamer.com/best-story-driven-video-games/.

24. *Tomb Raider III: Adventures of Lara Croft*, PlayStation (United States: Eidos Interactive, 1998).

25. Andrew Lazo and Libby John, "Learning from C.S. Lewis," Art & Faith Conversations, May 26, 2021, https://artandfaithconversations.libsyn.com/season-6-ep-12-learning-from-cs-lewis.

Chapter 8 Let There Be Tears

1. Naomi Ruth Floyd, "A Theology of the Blues & Belonging," Hutchmoot Podcast & Video, March 15, 2021, https://rabbitroom.com/2021/03/hutchmoot-podcast-video-a-theology-of-the-blues-belonging/.

2. Martin Luther King Jr., "Martin Luther King at the Berlin Jazz Fest in 1964," Jazz in Europe, January 21, 2019, https://jazzineurope.mfmmedia.nl/2019/01/martin-luther-king-at-the-berlin-jazz-fest-in-1964/.

3. Martin Luther King Jr., "Martin Luther King."

4. Martin Luther King Jr., "Martin Luther King."

5. Amy Vlodarski, "Musical Holocaust Memorials: Classical Music," Music and the Holocaust, accessed March 8, 2022, https://holocaustmusic.ort.org/memory/memorials/.

6. Nicholas Cannariato, "'How Shostakovich Changed My Mind' Touches On The Music-Body Connection," North Country Public Radio, May 17,

2019, https://www.northcountrypublicradio.org/news/npr/724274504/how
-shostakovich-changed-my-mind-touches-on-the-music-body-connection.

7. Music and the Holocaust, "Neuengamme," Music and the Holocaust, accessed March 26, 2022, https://holocaustmusic.ort.org/places/camps/cen tral-europe/neuengamme/.

8. Nicholas Cannariato, "'How Shostakovich Changed My Mind.'"

9. Naomi Ruth Floyd, "A Theology of the Blues & Belonging," (emphasis mine).

Chapter 9 Let There Be Breath

1. American Lung Association, "Inhale Air, Exhale Music," American Lung Association, September 20, 2019, https://www.lung.org/blog/inhale -air-exhale-music.

Chapter 10 Let There Be Movement

1. Joao Medeiros, "How Intel Gave Stephen Hawking a Voice," *Wired*, January 13, 2015, https://www.wired.com/2015/01/intel-gave-stephen-hawking -voice/.

2. "Primera Bailarina – Ballet en Nueva York – Años 60 – Música para Despertar," YouTube video, 3:16, posted by "Música para Despertar," October 30, 2020, https://www.youtube.com/watch?v=owb1uWDg3QM.

Chapter 11 Let There Be Silence

1. *Sound of Metal*, directed by Darius Marder (Culver City, CA: Amazon Studios; Los Angeles: Caviar, 2020), DVD.

2. Alicia Britt Chole, *Anonymous: Jesus' Hidden Years . . . and Yours* (Nashville: Thomas Nelson, 2006), 2–3.

3. Renita J. Weems, *Listening for God* (New York: Simon & Schuster, 1999), 25–26.

4. Jennifer Dukes Lee, *Growing Slow* (Grand Rapids: Zondervan, 2021), xx.

Chapter 12 Let There Be Thought

1. Robert E. Coleman, *The Master Plan of Evangelism* (Grand Rapids: Revell, 2010), 21 (emphasis mine).

2. Morgan Harper Nichols, *Forty Days on Being a Five* (Downers Grove, IL: InterVarsity, 2021), 8.

3. Jackie C. Horne, *Conversations with Madeleine L'Engle*. E-book ed. (University Press of Mississippi, 2018), Google Books, 74.

4. Faith & Leadership, "Makoto Fujimura: The Function of Art," Faith & Leadership, May 9, 2011, https://faithandleadership.com/makoto-fujimura -function-art.

Chapter 13 Let There Be Fellowship

1. *The Lord of the Rings: The Fellowship of the Ring*, "The Council of Elrond."
2. *Willy Wonka & The Chocolate Factory,* directed by Mel Stuart (Burbank, CA: Warner Bros. Pictures, 1971).
3. *Sherlock Holmes: A Game of Shadows,* directed by Guy Ritchie (Burbank, CA: Warner Bros. Pictures, 2011).
4. *The Avengers*, directed by Joss Whedon (Burbank, CA: Marvel Studios; Los Angeles: Paramount Pictures, 2012).
5. *Robin Hood,* directed by Wolfgang Reitherman (Burbank, CA: Walt Disney Productions, 1973).
6. C. S. Lewis, *C. S. Lewis The Screwtape Letters.* Directed by Max McLean, July 13, 2019, Belk Theater at Blumenthal Performing Arts Center, Charlotte.
7. L'Engle, *Walking on Water*, 14.
8. *The Lord of the Rings: The Fellowship of the Ring.*
9. Suzanne Collins, *The Hunger Games* (New York: Scholastic Press, 2008).
10. *Sherlock Holmes: A Game of Shadows.*
11. Peter Elbow, *Writing Without Teachers* (Oxford: Oxford University Press, 1998), 110–22.
12. *The Lord of the Rings: The Return of the King.*

Chapter 14 Let There Be Remembrance

1. This introduction has been adapted from a piece I wrote for the (in) courage blog. You can access it at https://www.incourage.me/2021/07/when-death-heals-your-fear-of-death.html.
2. Maurice Sendak and Eric Carle are famous authors / illustrators of children's books. They are best known for *Where the Wild Things Are* (New York: HarperCollins, 1963) and *The Very Hungry Caterpillar* (New York: Philomel Books, 1969), respectively.

Chapter 15 Let There Be Smallness

1. Neil Gaiman, "Neil Gaiman Teaches the Art of Storytelling," MasterClass, accessed March 7, 2022, https://www.masterclass.com/classes/neil-gaiman-teaches-the-art-of-storytelling.
2. Helena María Viramontes, "The Moths," *The Moths and Other Stories* (Houston: Arte Público Press, 1995), 27–32.
3. *Growing Floret*, season 1, episode 2, "Crossroads," Magnolia Network, aired on July 15, 2021, on Discovery Plus, 24:28.

Chapter 16 Let There Be Connection

1. Tom Standage, *Writing on the Wall: Social Media—The First 2,000 Years* (New York: Bloomsbury, 2013), 21–42.

2. Kristin Ohlson, "Reading the Writing on Pompeii's Walls," *Smithsonian*, July 26, 2010, https://www.smithsonianmag.com/history/reading-the-writing-on-pompeiis-walls-1969367/.

3. Tom Standage, *Writing on the Wall*, 53–54, 74–81.

Chapter 17 Let There Be Laughter

1. "Steve Martin Teaches Comedy: Official Trailer," YouTube video, 2:08, posted by "MasterClass," October 5, 2020, https://youtu.be/hP2o6CLT7mI.

2. *The Carol Burnett Show*, season 10, episode 8, "Show 1002," directed by Dave Powers, written by Roger Beatty, Elias Davis, and David Pollock, featuring Carol Burnett, Harvey Korman, and Vicki Lawrence, aired November 13, 1976, on CBS, https://www.youtube.com/watch?v=G8pPjlPWZAQ.

3. Joe Moran, "How Mockery Ate Comedy," *The Guardian*, August 7, 2009, https://www.theguardian.com/commentisfree/2009/aug/07/tv-comedy-humour-mockery.

Chapter 18 Let There Be Light

1. Lewis Carroll, *Alice's Adventures in Wonderland & Other Stories* (New York: Barnes & Noble Inc, 2018). This has also been published under the name *Alice in Wonderland* with other publishing companies.

2. E. B. White, *Charlotte's Web* (New York: Harper & Brothers, 1952).

Rachel Marie Kang is a New York native, born and raised just outside New York City. She is founder of The Fallow House (Fallow Ink) and her writing has been featured in *Christianity Today*, Proverbs 31 Ministries, and (in)courage. A mixed woman of African American, Native American (Ramapough Lenape Nation), Irish, and Dutch descent, she is a graduate of Nyack College with a Bachelor of Arts in English with Creative Writing. Rachel lives and writes in North Carolina with her husband and their two children. Connect with her at rachelmariekang.com and on social media @rachelmariekang.